Susann Vihma

PRODUCTS AS REPRESENTATIONS
- a semiotic and aesthetic study of design products

University of Art and Design Helsinki UIAH

1995

Publication series of the University of Art and Design Helsinki UIAH A 14
© 1995 Susann Vihma
Graphic design: Tarja Petrell
Cover photo: Taneli Eskola
English revision: Georgianna Oja

ISBN 951-9384-89-8
ISSN 0782-1832
Printed at Gummerus Kirjapaino Oy Jyväskylä 1995

Distribution:
University of Art and Design Helsinki UIAH
UIAH Information and Publishing Unit
Hämeentie 135 C, FIN-00560 Helsinki
Finland

CONTENTS

ACKNOWLEDGEMENTS

My thanks are due to Professor Ilkka Niiniluoto at the University of Helsinki. He read the very early drafts I wrote and has made valuable comments at all stages.

I am grateful to Associate Professor Victor Margolin, from the University of Illinois at Chicago, for his useful suggestions for improvements and encouraging attitude and to Professor Eero Tarasti, from the University of Helsinki, for his critical remarks and thoughtful ideas concerning the manuscript. I want to thank Professor Arto Haapala, from the University of Helsinki, especially for his comments on the aesthetic part of the research. I have also benefited from the remarks made by Pentti Määttänen on the semiotic sign.

A positive interest towards my study has been shown by many persons at the University of Art and Design Helsinki UIAH; I want to thank them all. Especially, I want to express my gratitude to the Rector, Yrjö Sotamaa, and to Associate Professor Yrjänä Levanto for their support. Professor Severi Parko offered useful comments on the manuscript. In addition, in my teaching work, I have been able to discuss issues concerning my object of study. I am grateful for these opportunities to the students and to those who organized the study programmes, especially to Mariaana von Knorring, Raimo Nikkanen and Satu Tamminen. I am also indebted to the helpful attitudes of the library headed by Liisa Kemppi and of the data service personnel headed by Martti Lummaa.

I want to express my gratitude to Georgianna Oja, who revised the English version of the manuscript.

Finally, my very special thanks go to my husband, Tapani Vihma, for his comments and support.

INTRODUCTION

The representative function of design products has been studied very little because technical and ergonomic aspects have had priority in product development. When the representativeness of things has been studied, works of art have generally been dealt with. Typical everyday products have remained without attention, even though they also always represent something. Semioticians have developed analyses on representation, but they have usually examined products from the point of view of their cultural history, not from that of design (Bogatyrev 1936, Barthes 1954–56, Eco 1968 and 1979). They have also studied the products as symbols and as language-like systems. However, with the approach developed by Charles S. Peirce (*CP*, 1935–1966) already at the end of the last century, a product can be interpreted in many different ways as a sign, not merely as a symbol. Therefore Peirce's semiotics seems more suitable for the study of design products than other approaches do.

The purpose of this study was to examine the representative function of design products and apply Peirce's semiotic approach. The objective of the analysis of product examples was to illustrate their function as signs. I also studied aesthetic aspects of design because the question of whether a product is conceived as beautiful and elegant is associated with what it represents. My aim was to present how the interpretation of a product as a sign can be combined with its aesthetic appreciation (Walton 1970).

The form of the design product is an object for interpretation, not merely a property of the product. Problems related to design interpretation have seldom been studied. It was not until the 1980s that theories for product design were presented that accounted for a product's expression and meaning (Klöcker 1980, Oehlke 1982, Gros 1983, Krippendorff and Butter 1984, Buchanan 1989), even though such aspects have long been considered important in design thinking (Maldonado 1961, Gugelot 1962, Dorfles 1964, Schürer 1969, Archer 1974). Design studies can, however, be criticized as being too general in scope in that they strive to cover the entire field of design. Their broad approach does not allow enough space for the interpretation of a design product. The design product is only very narrowly examined because the study of its interpretation is restricted.

In my research I have discussed the constitution of the semiotic sign in the case of a design product and analysed its functions as a sign. This was an important starting point because the application of the concept of sign would otherwise lead the analysis of representation astray. Thereafter, I characterized different modes of reference of design products applying Peirce's distinction of iconic, indexical and symbolic signs. Accordingly, I have grouped the different modes of reference to analyse empirical sample material. I have chosen the following four design products from the market for closer examination: the steam iron, the exercise cycle, the telephone kiosk, and the bicycle helmet.

The research indicates that the application of the semiotic sign is an interesting conceptional tool for interpreting representational qualities. Especially iconic and indexical signs seem to structure representation in a new way from the design point of view. Of more general significance is the fact that a semiotic approach can provide concepts that explain the interaction between persons and artefacts.

qualities' (ICSID 1965, p.7), 'visual expression', 'aesthetic attributes' (Archer 1965 and 1974, p.79), and 'informative function' (Klöcker 1980, p.17). It is interesting to note that semantic and aesthetic features have been treated together and seem to be related.

In the following discussion I use the term 'design' instead of 'industrial design' even though industrially produced artefacts in particular are examined. I do this deliberately because 'design' is an activity in which different aspects can be emphasized, not only the aspect of production. 'Designers' can have divergent tasks (not only those related to industry) and are often interested in applying their skills to a broad scope of projects. Successful designers of today, as well as the prominent designers of yesterday, are generally versatile planners who only seldom restrict their activities to one type of product (Dresser, Hoffman, Loewy, Gugelot, Sottsass, Wirkkala). It seems to me that the crossing of traditional professional boundaries in design, as well as the indifferent attitude towards them, has been advantageous for designers.

The design product

The object of this study is the 'design product', which is a term commonly used in German, English, and Swedish literature on design. With it, I am not referring to the models or prototypes that are common stages in a product development process, nor to the designer's sketches for a product. The design product in this study has been accepted for production and is on the market for sale. It is called a design product because a designer has undisputably contributed to the planning process. Defined in this way, the design product excludes many industrially produced artefacts on the market. This statement does not mean, however, that these artefacts cannot become 'design products'. A person with education in design has simply not been employed in their planning or taken part in the product development team.

Electric appliances, products in heating and ventilation engineering, children's toys, street furniture, gifts and souvenirs are common products that are not always 'design products' according to my definition. Principles and goals of 'design' have not (yet) been applied in the planning and realization of these artefacts. Instead technical and commercial aspects in particular have been considered.

For reading ease, I have used the word 'product' instead of 'design product' in the following discussion. In spite of the broad and varying meanings of the term, I think that the reader has been introduced to the object of this study and my use will not lead to disturbing misunderstandings. The term 'product' should be understood as the outcome of a design process.

The form of a product

A designer is not a mere inventor of forms (kein reiner Form-Erfinder), as Gugelot (1962, p.47) pointed out. In many definitions of design, the use of the word 'form' is avoided so that the outer form, appearance or surface of the product will not be given too much attention in people's conceptions of design. The avoidance and understatement of 'form' can be seen as anxiety towards a too superficial conception of design as mere styling. 'Form' in connection with design can also create the wrong conception in people's minds about the work of designers. Design can be considered a kind of cosmetic finish given to technical construction.

In his analysis on visual perception Rudolf Arnheim (1974, p.43, 92 and 97) conceives objects as having shapes and forms. The visual shape of an object is largely determined by its outer boundaries, but not only by these boundaries. In addition, a structural skeleton created in perception determines it. When shape, at the same time, represents something, it also has form. Sibylle Kicherer (1987, p.32), on the other hand, has criticized the use of the concept of form in design and prefers the use of 'Gestalt' instead. In her view, 'form' refers too easily to external coverage and surface. Therefore, she conceived form only as part of a broader concept, the Gestalt (figure 2).

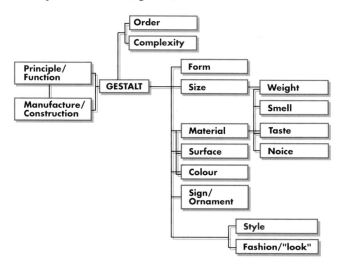

Figure 2. The form is part of the Gestalt (translated from Kicherer 1987, p.33. See also Escherle 1986 p.38).

In this study, I have tried to problematize a one-dimensional conception of 'form'. If 'form' is something other than the outer surface and coverage of a product, then what is it? I conceive the form of a product as taking part in the perception process, in which both the physical object and perceiving subject are regarded. Accordingly, the problem of form does not simply relate to the coverage or the physical form of a material product and its shape. Neither is form only an idea in the perceiver's mind.

Freedom of form

In product design, there are different grades of freedom of form. The gradation has been understood as being dependent on the technical complexity of a product, which also relates to its use. Products have been placed on a curve expressing grades of freedom of form (figure 3). Complex products are, accordingly, mainly capital goods. Their form is more restricted than that of consumer goods.

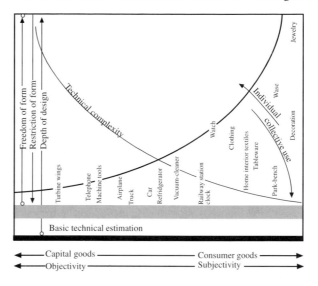

Figure 3. Examples of freedom grades of form (translated from Klöcker 1980, p.72).

The products in figure 3 serve to illustrate the idea of freedom grades. Design plays an important part and has more meaning for products with greater freedom of form. In other words, there is more room for variation in form without technical restrictions. For example, a telephone is placed on the curve where its form is highly restricted. In the figure, the telephone exemplifies a complex product permitting only a small variation in form. Today, fifteen years later, there are many telephone models on the market. It seems that the telephone's place on the curve has shifted. Technical complexity does not seem to influence the place on the curve directly and does not necessarily limit the freedom of form in design in a fixed way. However, this conception has prevailed for a long time in design. (See, e.g., Lannoch 1983, p.28).

Optimal form

Technology has been conceived as the main determinant of a product's form. It has even seemed possible to construct an optimal form. However, such a concept cannot be generalized to all types of products (Schürer 1969, p.15; Steadman 1979, p.243). If an optimal form is possible to construct at all, it seems to suit only a small number of products. In design literature, only a few examples can be found, such as the crane hook and a ship's propeller (Archer 1956, p.15–16).

Philip Steadman (1979) has analysed the relationship between design thinking and concepts in natural philosophy, such as those of Lamarck and Darwin. The goals of design have been formulated with nature as a model, as is also common-place in other types of cultural studies (Niiniluoto 1985).

The optimal form derives from the concept that the forms of artefacts are similar to natural forms. Goethe thought that all forms of plants spring from one original plant (Urpflanze). Similarly the forms of artefacts were conceived as springing from original forms. Mechanical development was conceived to be similar to that of nature (a comparison with Darwin's theory). The aesthetic features of artefacts and natural objects were therefore considered to be similar. It has also been thought that all forms of artefacts can be reduced to a few original basic forms. In the 1920s the so-called Purists, Le Corbusier and Amédée Ozenfant, classified objects in 'types'. Products such as household utensils and tools have original type forms, which gradually change with technical development. Finally the forms develop into perfect standards. Figure 4 illustrates this process.

The Purists thought that the development of standard type forms would necessarily lead to a reduced geometric form, which would finally lead to an anonymous form without references.

A reduced and 'natural' product form is a kind of design ideal in the Functionalist tradition, although Functionalism in the 1920s was not a coherent and strictly defined trend. However, functional and technological aspects were

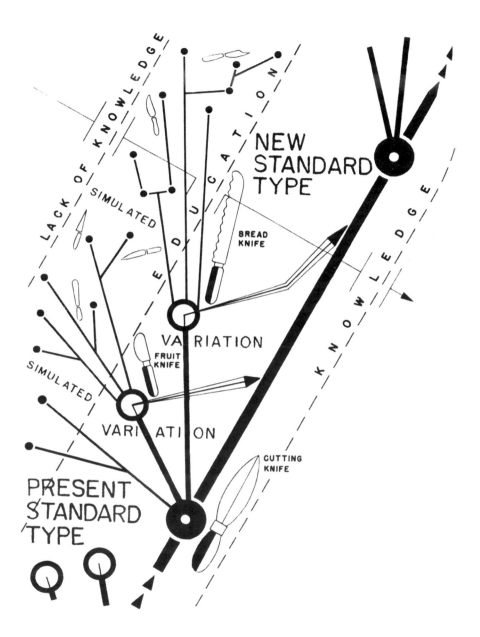

Figure 4. Development of standard types of artefacts, as illustrated by Kiesler in the 1930s (Steadman 1979, p.164).

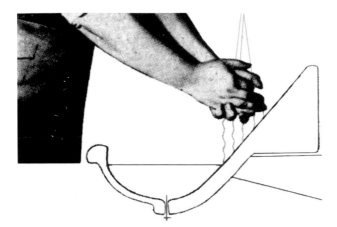

commonly stressed in Functionalism. In addition, the embodiment of the object's 'inner structure' was important. A functionally 'honest', practical, open and hygienic product was the ideal (Mikkola 1978, p.50; Mikkola et al. 1980; Sparke 1987a, p.130) as can be seen in figure 5.

Still in the late 1940s, Functionalist ideals prevailed in design. If these ideals are applied in a strict sense, Functionalism is easily reduced to a mere stylistic mannerism. Criticism towards them began to grow in the late 1960s, and the discussion about the crisis of Functionalism started (Schürer 1969, p.13; Mikkola 1978, p.52; Selle 1978, p.198; Ahola 1980, p.70-71; Sparke 1987a, p.214).

Ten criteria for good form

Design products have been evaluated annually in connection with the Die gute Industrieform fair in Hannover in Germany, since 1953, and awards for outstanding international design have been given on the basis of the evaluation by a jury. A catalogue of the awarded products has been published and widely distributed. Herbert Lindinger made a list of nine criteria for this evaluation in 1982. One year later they became ten and were slightly modified (Lindinger 1983 and 1989). Eight of the ten refer to the use and technical properties of a design product. These are requirements for practicability, safety, a long useful life, ergonomics, originality of form, relation to environment, energy sparing and visualization. The ninth concerns the quality of design (with seven subcriteria). The subcriteria of design quality include, for example, principles of visual composition such as exactitude, clarity (no visual disturbance), unambiguity, consistency and logical design. In addition, good design should be aesthetically meaningful, which is explained as an arrangement in harmony with manufacture, assembly and maintenance. The tenth criterion concerns the stimulation of sense and intellect. In short, it means a form which can lead to an identification, but, in fact, it covers a vast field of qualities.

However, both the criteria and the design juries have been criticized (Gugelot 1962, p.47; Beuck and Jaspersen 1983; Kicherer 1987, p.46). Many believe that the juries' conception of design has been narrow, even though the criteria were loosely formulated. The criteria are sometimes so general that they seem self-evident when published. They have, however, been interpreted narrowly, and this interpretation has led to the formation of a style. The same features have been stressed over and over again by the juries. Thus the design awards have had a normative effect on design and have directed good taste. Models for good form have been created, and these models have had a restrictive influence on design.

Semiotics and design

Representational qualities of design products have been studied in psychology, semiotics and aesthetics. Petr Bogatyrev (1936) wrote that products such as clothes can function as material objects and signs at the same time. In addition to their practical functioning, they also have, for example, an ideological role. In their ideological function products are signs that refer to something other than the material product and its practical functions.

> A phenomenon of material reality has become a phenomenon of ideological reality: a thing has changed into a sign.
> (Bogatyrev 1936, p.13)

In the 1960s, designers began to speak about the semantic quality and the communicative features of products and the products' messages. At that time Roland Barthes (1954–1956) analysed everyday objects, and Umberto Eco (1968) studied architectural objects with the help of a semiotic approach.

Earlier, in 1937–1938, Charles Morris taught philosophy and provided students of design with general theoretical knowledge at the New Bauhaus in Chicago. He was invited to teach by László Moholy-Nagy, who had been Form master at the Bauhaus in Germany. The pedagogical aim of Morris was to connect art, science and technology and inform the students in all of these fields (Hahn und Engelbrecht 1987, p.260; Findeli 1991; Poisson 1994). As a semiotician, Morris is also well-known for his division of analyses into syntax, semantics and pragmatics (Morris 1971; Niiniluoto 1980, p.90; Sebeok et al. 1986, p.566). His philosophical approach belongs to pragmatism, which was influenced by Charles Peirce. In their thinking special emphasis is placed on the 'pragmatic dimension' of an analysis and the importance of taking the interpreter (or interpreting community) into account (Niiniluoto 1980, p.94). Morris' approach may have influenced conceptions of the relationship between semiotics and design. The Morris approach seems to have been more familiar to Maldonado (1961) and Krippendorff (1992), for example, than other semiotic approaches were.

A designer of well-known products of Braun, Kodak and Telefunken, Hans Gugelot, designed a television apparatus in 1956. The form was mainly based on ergonomic and technological considerations. In spite of the rational emphasis in his design, the result was in his view, not only an objectively definable form, but also an expression, which Gugelot called its physiognomy. The product expresses as a sign, according to Gugelot; it shows how it can be used and how it functions. (Compare Dorfles 1964, p.30.) Its form exhibits, for example, a spot for grasping or winding, a direction for the winding and so on. Bringing out an expressive quality in relation to use is then an essential task of designers.

Designers' interest in semiotics and semiotic applications began in the 1950s at the Ulm School (Hochschule für Gestaltung Ulm, 1955–1968). The goal of education at the Ulm School was a well-educated designer able to communicate with experts of other fields. For this purpose contacts were sought to different, especially new fields of knowledge. Design should benefit from the most recent scientific achievements (Kellner and Poessnecker 1978, Metsä-Ketelä 1991). Tomás Maldonado and Gui Bonsiepe taught semiotic theory and published design applications of semiotics (Lindinger 1987). Bonsiepe (1961, p.19–34) studied communicative features of pictures by applying a semiotic analysis. He used advertising pictures as examples. At that time, designers lacked conceptual means for any proper analysis or evaluation of pictures (and products). There was only loud criticism from professional designers, and the criticism was not based on any explicit analysis, which, in Bonsiepe's view, is a requirement for competent criticism. A well-argued critique needs analysis, and the analysis, in turn, requires a qualified description of its object. Martin Krampen, student and teacher at the Ulm School (Maldonado 1961, p.46; Lindinger 1987, p.276), later applied semiotics in his pedagogical work at the University of Arts in Berlin (Hochschule der Künste Berlin). (See Krampen 1979 and 1986.)

Abraham Moles and Max Bense, both teachers at the Ulm School, developed semiotic and aesthetic approaches thought to be applicable to design. Bense (1971) applied Charles Peirce's semiotics to develop a design theory that could be used to analyse design products and advertising pictures. His theory aimed at linking an aesthetic design concept to the semiotic as well. In Bense's model (figure 6), a design product has four dimensions.

The material dimension, the hyletics, includes the analysis of a product's material qualities. The syntactic dimension includes the technical construction and functioning of the product, but not yet its form. According to Bense the semantic dimension, the morphetics, includes the product form (die industrielle

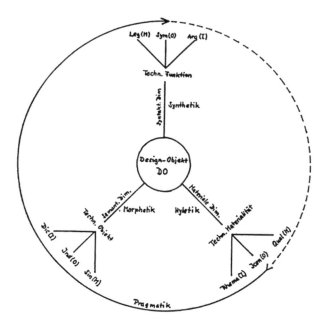

Figure 6. Four semiotic dimensions of a design product, as illustrated by Bense (1971, p.81).

Produktform). The form is distinguished as a dimension of its own, and thus the semantics seems to center around the form of a product.

All three dimensions include a different triadic sign relation. A product has specific signs on each dimension which characterizes it. The product has a sign relation in its material dimension, another in its syntactic dimension, and a third in its semantic dimension. The characteristic sign for the material dimension is the icon, for the syntactic it is the symbol, and for the semantic the index.

The pragmatic dimension is conceived as embracing the other dimensions and as resulting from them. The fourth dimension does not have a 'traditional Peircean' sign relation at all. It is like a total dimension that cannot be approached by analysing a triadic sign relation. However, the model seems to fall apart in spite of its embracing pragmatic circle. The vast pragmatic field cannot stop the break-up. Neither do the divergent sign relations of the dimensions any longer clarify the object of study. Material iconic signs and syntactic symbols were not explained by Bense, but were only briefly stated as such.

Roland Barthes (1967) introduced a semiotic model, the system of syntagmatic units. Products and their details form a system. Menus and portions of food form a 'food system', clothes form a 'garment system', and so forth. A dress, for example, can be examined as a system of details such as the collar, epaulets, pockets and sleeves. The detail, such as the fastening of a dress, conveys semantic support that is variation in a detail such as a button, zipper, tape, snap, concealed fastening and the like. Changing the semantic support changes the meaning of the dress simultaneously. And its references and interpretations are changed. In other words, when the semantic support is changed, the dress as a sign also changes. This model seems practical for an analysis of a material product. The semantic support of the detail (the variation of a collar, the collar model) is defined first. When the support is changed, the semantics of the whole dress changes as well. This is not surprising. The practicality of the analysis would rather be that by changing the semantic support of a detail in one direction, a person learns how to change another dress in the same direction. Later on, details could be designed into another object with the same semantic results. Through this process a person could systematically classify semantic variations of products. First, however, a semantic support of a detail has to be defined in this analysis.

Criticism of applied semiotics

It seems to me that semiotic concepts are included in current design literature to validate the presentation or to show the academic expertise of the writer (as, e.g., Heufler 1988, p.18, Manzini 1991, p.52). On the other hand, critics of semiotics like Sless (1986, p.179) call the approach fashionable, trivialize its problem and avoid discussing it. In each case, semiotics is simply not examined. Only a brief and superficial image of semiotics is transmitted. Semiotic application has, in my view, suffered from such treatment. Another hindrance to application could be the formalized presentations of the semiotic sign, for example, by Bense (1971). It should be noted that only a few attempts have been made to apply semiotics to design. The concepts in these applications may seem strange and ambiguous at first. They also vary from study to study. Familiar concepts are used, but they may have a specific semiotic shade of meaning. New terms are invented and used by researchers. An attempt should therefore be made to avoid mystifying semiotics with obscure concepts. Vulgar semiotics applies concepts arbitrarily without connecting them to earlier studies or any explicated philosophical approach. Concepts are used in a vague or snobbish way. At most such a text may include semiotic terms. Commonly used terms, among others, are language, communication, meaning, code, sign, icon, metaphor, symbol, message, signal and information.

Information theory is sometimes mentioned in design studies (Maldonado 1961, Moles 1968, Garnich 1968, Bense 1971, Klöcker 1980, Maser 1981). It is a mathematical theory used, for example, in information psychology and information aesthetics. Information theory examines the concept 'information', the transmission and change of information in the perception process. Moles regards information as a measurable entity. Thomas Ellinger has developed a mathematical application called the 'product information theory', which Klöcker used in his study on design products. I am not aiming at a mathematical analysis in my study. Therefore, I shall not discuss the applications of information theory any further.

Aesthetics in design

Aesthetics is a field closer and more familiar to design than semiotics. Gregor Paulsson and Nils Paulsson (1956, p.78) have illuminated the question of what is usually meant by the aesthetics of a product. It can be exemplified, for example, by an old Chinese porcelain bowl, which no longer serves a practical purpose. The bowl has been put in a museum vitrine. The 'pure beauty', the form and colour, of the thing can be perceived. The bowl exhibits what Bense (1971, p.65–66) called an 'aesthetic state', which is experienced by the perceiver, and in this case it may represent an aesthetic ideal as well. Other potters try to reach this ideal and will, accordingly, make bowls for the museum vitrine. In this way, Paulsson and Paulsson distinguish between the practical and aesthetic use of a thing. Aesthetic things are designed to be exhibited and for their own sake, rather than to serve any practical purpose. (See also Moles 1968, p.131.) This conception of the aesthetic seems suitable in the marketing and sale of products, for which the appearance on the store shelf is very important, along with the display. The practical use of the product may be subordinated to its appearance.

Maser (1987, p.95.), on the other hand, divides the field of aesthetics into free arts and useful arts. According to Functionalist aesthetics, the technical structure and function of a product should be stressed, and appearance is considered secondary. Good aesthetic quality in design is achieved by solving material, technical and ergonomic problems in an efficient and economic manner. An illuminating example from design history is the debate in Vienna in the beginning of this century between Adolf Loos and the designers of Wiener Werkstätte. The different viewpoints of this discussion clearly present, in my view, the functionalistic approach to design aesthetics, in which the beauty of a product follows from the fulfillment of its functional aspects.

Meaning in design

The study by Csikszentmihalyi and Rochberg-Halton (1981) on the meaning of things is interesting because its objects were everyday products. Therefore, it is a study about design products as well. Csikszentmihalyi and Rochberg-Halton noted, to begin with, that products have not been studied much in the social sciences and psychology, and in anthropological studies, a product is usually conceived as a symbol and as part of a social activity or ritual. The product is studied as merely a means of interpersonal relations or inside a person's mental processes as meaning. Then the products themselves become marginal objects of study. In the investigations by Sigmund Freud, such as his Interpretation of Dreams from 1900, the umbrella and the walking stick were not objects of interpretation as such. The object of study was a person's conception of these things. A similar treatment appears in the analyses by Donald Winnicott (1971, p.47), which included 'transitional objects' such as children's blankets and soft toys. The phenomena in the analyses were projections of inner psychic activity. 'Mental schemes' in these theories were conceived a priori and the product environment functioned merely as support of mental structures. The thing itself was supposed to be neutral. Another disadvantage in psychological studies is the conception of culture as a static system instead of as an active process of interaction.

Csikszentmihalyi and Rochberg-Halton considered things as actively partaking in the socializing process of human beings because they embody models for social roles. Things in use are able to embody social goals and people's expectations. But this ability is usually too obvious to be considered.

The starting point of Csikszentmihalyi and Rochberg-Halton (1981, p.43) was the conception of man as being what he does. Things are subordinated to the doing, but they influence the formation of the self. To understand the relationship between the human being and the thing is, therefore, important. The relationship is interactive. The thing itself contributes actively to the meaning process. A thing is not just a passive projection; it is able to convey meaning through its own inherent qualities. Any object can convey meaning. It seems, however, that some things are more inclined to do so than others. Both the physical properties of a thing and the values given to the thing affect the formation of meaning.

Csikszentmihalyi and Rochberg-Halton (1981, p.50 and 139) conceived the meaning of things as sign processes in which meanings are created. Their empirical material consisted of domestic objects and milieus. The conception of the self is nowadays also formed by means of consumer goods. For example, leisure-time equipment embodies what people are able to do and, thus, who they are. Domestic items express a kind of conception of the home and a kind of activity in the home. Similarly, domestic organization can be conceived as a signifying pattern. Meanings are concretized in things and expressed in an atmosphere created by the things. Objects may refer to a signifying pattern broader than themselves, to people's conception of the world. But a thing does not coincide with simply one specific message. When a person highly regards the stereo equipment, the meaning of the thing cannot be directly concluded from this regard. Listening to music may refer to the self and to the feeling of joy experienced through the use of the equipment. But the relationship may include meanings that surpass the individual because it connects the listener to social contexts and cultural values, which should also be clarified.

An interesting result of the study by Csikszentmihalyi and Rochberg-Halton is the fact that things are not appreciated because of the material comfort they provide, but because of the 'information' they transmit (i.e., information about the owner and relations to other people). Kinship information transmitted by the product is especially important, rather than information about ethnic, political, national or religious relations.

One of the most interesting aspects of the study by Csikszentmihalyi and Rochberg-Halton, from the point of view of my study, is that things are conceived as signs, as objectified forms of psychic energy. A person can experience objects subjectively and objectively at the same time and relate the experience with the properties of the thing. This process refers to the sign function. Two entities are combined. The Greeks called it 'sym-ballein', to throw together.

Before I proceed to examine other earlier studies on design products closer, I would like to point to the fact that a designer, when planning, often 'studies' the product with the aid of background material, drawings and mock-ups. The aim is to find a proper solution to a form problem. This kind of professional analysis was published in design literature and in relation to design exhibitions especially in the 1960s. The articles analyse qualities of a particular product. However, general conclusions for design are not drawn in these analyses, so that the results could have been applied in other cases (except Rams and Ullman 1984/85). No theory has been developed on the basis of these articles. Thus it can be concluded that it is not even sensible to construct general principles in design. A design task would, each time, consist of an original series of events (Buchanan 1992, p.16).

On the other hand, there has been a need for general principles and criteria in design in order to, for example, evaluate good form and to educate designers. As noted earlier, hitherto the criteria used have seemed too general. Products can be evaluated only roughly according to them, and the evaluation depends on the opinions of the jury members.

Evidently, the material gathered for one design project does not necessarily serve the needs of another. New data have to be collected. But, eventually, data that can be useful later will probably be gathered from various fields of knowledge. A design consultant may have a long-lasting business relationship with a company. The same kind of products are designed over a long period of time. Knowledge acquired during this time does not necessarily vary much; instead it expands and cumulates. The designer may have specialized, and specialization will support this tendency to expand the database and collect material more systematically. The designer may begin to develop conceptual bases and methods for the application of knowledge. Thus the conditions for a discussion on design theory seem promising.

Previous analyses

In the following discussion, I have used chronological order to introduce design studies that have contributed to my study. Factors that influenced industrial products were, at first, mostly technological and economic (Schürer 1969). Products were, therefore, analysed from a technical and material point of view. (See also Black 1972, p.178; Oehlke 1982, p.5.)

In the 1960s, more emphasis was placed on the visual quality of products. Barnes' article (1962, p.20–30) gives a good example, when it describes a case study of the design of electronic equipment for hospital use. The responsibility of its design was given to a team under the leadership of Tomás Maldonado. The objective was to standardize the equipment range and simplify production. At the same time it was possible to change the visual image of the products (figure 7).

Figure 7. Old and new equipment (Barnes 1962, p.32).

The commission also included the design of the company's logo type. The aim was similarly to clarify and simplify the design. As can be concluded from figure 8, the visual image was changed radically. The nature of this change and its possible effects were, however, not discussed in Barnes' article.

Figure 8. The old and new logotype (Barnes 1962, p.30).

The example shows how technological and related economic aspects have dominated design. The product's relationship to someone's use was considered only from an ergonomic point of view. As such the analysis was incomplete because it lacked the study of other factors that could have affected the visual quality of the products. Or, possibly, designers may have thought at that time that the problems of design can be solved by applying sufficiently sophisticated technological and ergonomic knowledge.

The example is interesting also because the team was headed by a highly esteemed theorist, pedagogue and designer, Tomás Maldonado. He was one of the first to try to integrate new fields of knowledge, such as information theory and semiotics, into design and design pedagogy. It can, therefore, be assumed that Maldonado could have had other thoughts about the commission as well, but designers and critics in general were not yet able to interpret and deal with them. Such thoughts did not reach Barnes and his article.

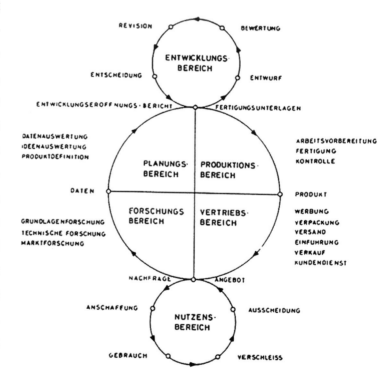

Figure 9. Functional fields of product-influencing factors (Schürer 1969, p.29).

Arnold Schürer (1969) has examined the influence of various factors on a design product and provided support to the preceding discussion. Influencing factors appear in six functional fields divided into sections along with a product's life cycle. The six fields are consumption, research, design, product development, production and trade (figure 9).

Schürer's empirical material consists of products from the well-known German electrotechnical company AEG (Allgemeine Elektricitäts-Gesellschaft), which exemplifies typical technical development. The products are especially interesting from a design point of view. (See also Sparke 1987b.) They change continuously with the possibilities of both the producer and the users (figure 10).

Not only technological and economic considerations but also subjective assessments influence the product. By 'subjective assessment' Schürer (1969, p.30) means non-measurable factors like expectations and wishes, opinions and attitudes. The product is designed in respect to them, too. Knowledge about the subjective factors is acquired by means of marketing research.

Figure 10. Water boilers by AEG between 1900-1960 (Schürer 1969, appendix III).

Subjective factors do not only affect the fields of practical use or technical function, but appear already in earlier phases of planning, when the product requirements are defined. In product development, most of the influencing factors are of this kind, subjectively assigned. The design phase in particular includes subjective assessments because, in addition to technical and economic factors, also factors in relation to the environment and users are defined. Even if subjective factors can be seen as influencing design, they may not always be considered to improve visual appearance. A subjective judgement may only concern a detail of the product, and it may not change or improve the product as a whole.

Subjective factors, a topic which Schürer discussed, should be seen as interacting with technical and economic factors. Technical knowledge and improvement affect people's expectations, and people's expectations affect, in turn, technical solutions.

Klöcker's analysis of design products

For a start, Ingo Klöcker (1980) analysed design as a professional activity. Then he introduced design-related disciplines. With the help of these disciplines he developed a systematic approach for his analysis of a design product. He classified criteria first according to the relevant disciplines. Then he grouped the criteria in another way, semiotically into semantic, syntactic and pragmatic criteria. Finally he applied the method in his analysis of examples of design products: a front panel of a radio set, an oil heater, a telephone and a razor.

Product development and design in general show a tendency towards the optimization of form (Klöcker 1980, p.139). Optimization seems always to lead to a reduction and simplification of the product. A contrasting tendency is the addition of information and an increase in readability. Klöcker calls it the tendency towards differentiation. Readability, and with it, increased ease of use are achieved by

Figure 11. A mature form exemplified by the Braun razor sixtant from 1962 (Klöcker 1980, p.126).

designing visual and tactile guides to the product form. There are, then, continuously two contrasting tendencies interacting in design, the optimization towards a reduced and easily perceivable form and the informative tendency with various details added to the form. A third tendency aiming at order can also be distinguished. This is a tendency aiming at a product that is a coherent whole in which functional, ergonomic and semiotic order is apparent. Compromises have been successfully made between these three tendencies in the cases Klöcker chose as his examples.

Klöcker (1980, p.136) concludes, on the basis of the analysis of his material, that a form that has reached maturity can no longer be improved by means of differentiation. The designer's task would then be to add superfluous details to a perfect form. An example of a mature product form is the Braun razor sixtant (figure 11).

The subject matter of Klöcker's analysis is close to my study. Therefore, both his approach and his systematic analysis seemed to me to be a promising starting point. The fact that it also included an application to concrete design products increased its promising usefulness for my purposes. The benefit of Klöcker's study was, however, not the material, analysis or application. The study was interesting because of its attempt to combine different fields of knowledge in the design context. Klöcker not only made a list of different qualities, he examined their internal relations and order. Design was characterized by such a complex combination in his applications, too. And this very feature of complexity of design was considered particularly difficult. Many lists of requirements have been published, but an attempt at combining different qualities has, to my knowledge, not been made as thoroughly as by Klöcker.

There is room for criticism of Klöcker's approach in spite of its obvious merits. My critical remarks concern the background material of the study (Teil 5 Anhang). Especially its semiotic part was not useful. Semiotic literature is much more complex and differentiated than Klöcker's brief review would have people believe. Very shortly he presented a thin semiotic basis for his analysis and did not present any arguments to support his application. Many questions thus remain unanswered and they hamper further application. In addition, he treated a design product too much like a two-dimensional drawing. He presented semantic features before syntactic features, but did not give any reason for this order. Neither did he mention why he left material criteria outside the scope of his analysis. He listed a total of 15 semantic criteria. Five of them were not used in the analysis, and he did not give any explanation concerning their possible unsuitability. Also his treatment of aesthetics in design can be critisised for being too narrow. After an aesthetic approach to design has been introduced, one can assume that also aesthetic criteria will be included in the application. But Klöcker left them out. All in all, the application is flexible with regard to the different product examples, but Klöcker did not point out the benefits of the flexibility. Therefore, the application may seem incoherent or incomplete. The merit of the application is its fluent verbal presentation, which concentrates on relevant features of the products. His informal way with description makes the reading easy and interesting.

Klöcker's thesis covered a vast field of product-related features and structured the analysis of design products. In the discussion, he stated that a verbal description of a product remains inaccurate. Although he did not develop a mathematical and measurable means of analysis, he was able to draw some general conclusions about the products in his application. He referred to further development which would make the analysis more precise with the help of a mathematical presentation. He did not deliberate about how he would proceed. The mere mentioning of it is, however, revealing, because he may later attempt a systemization of design on the basis of a formal method. Such an attempt would require exact mathematical criteria for design products. Once the qualities of a product have been formalized, it would be possible to set up numeric criteria for it and thereafter also for products in general, perhaps even for the design. Klöcker was aware of the limits and weaknesses of such attempts. As a warning example he may have thought of Rolf Garnich's (1968) analysis of product form by means of mathematics. Its weakness from a design point of view was the complex operations of even rather simple product forms (porcelain tea pots). Designers do not usually have a mathematical education sufficient for such calculations or for an application of the operations to design practice.

Semantics of product language

It was obvious from the literature survey that the analysis of semantic features of design products is intricate. However, semantic issues have awakened vast interest among designers. Semantics is often mentioned, but its characterization has remained on a level that is too general. In the 1980s the interest resulted in design studies such as those of Klöcker (1980), Oehlke (1982), Gros (1983), Smets (1987), Väkevä (1987), Kicherer (1987), Athavankar (1990) and Bush (1990). After 1984 'product semantics' spread in the design world especially because of the articles in the American design magazine innovation edited by Klaus Krippendorff and Reinhart Butter in the spring of 1984. Current textbooks and exhibition books on design include product semantics as a special topic (Bürdek 1991, Jeudy 1993, Quarante 1994).

A common feature in these writings is the product regarded as a means of communication. Special emphasis is given to informative qualities and to the communicative relationship between the product and its user. What a product expresses is mediated by product language according to Gros (1983, p.63). Another common feature of the aforementioned studies is care for user abilities in communicative interaction. The product should, accordingly, be seen in the context of use, not as a separate technical construction.

People usually understand everyday things only partially, especially if they include mechanisms or electronic control. Therefore, design has taken on a new role. The designer's task is no longer the same as in the 1960s, as illustrated in Barnes' example. Designers cannot limit themselves to reducing the product form to promote technological rationalization. Although reduction may increase readability, it no longer suffices. 'Messages' for the user must be designed.

Jochen Gros (1983, 1984 and 1987) has developed a theory of product language close to semiotics to help the designer accomplish the new task. A designer should aim at understanding product language better to be able to improve his design. In addition a designer should be able to say something in this language. In stressing the content of product language, the domain of design philosophy is approached (i.e., a philosophy of values, feelings and patterns of thought in everyday life). It is expressed by products. Without a design philosophy designers cannot produce good product language. They will not succeed in achieving the expression wished for. They will reach nothing by means of design if enough is not known about the content of the message.

The theory of product language can be divided in two parts, the formal and the semantic (Gros 1983, p.63). The theory is not yet complete because the formal part has not yet been published. Gros himself has been more interested in the semantics of product language and Dieter Mankau had planned to analyse the formal aesthetic, the non-semantic part.

The most important concept in the theory is 'self-explanation' of a product (Selbsterklärung). In design practice this property is regarded as a quality that is difficult to describe and design. It is a nonverbal expression by which the product exhibits its practical function. It cannot therefore be a property of the product only. Rather, it is a relationship between the product and the user, a sign (figure 12). 'Self-explanation' is a sign that refers to the practical functions of the product. For example, by designing the grooves of a handle a designer can express how to grasp a product (Gros 1984a, p.12). A designer must master some form of product language to be able to embody the self explanation of a product. (See also Bürdek 1985.)

'Self explanation' points directly to a property (2a in figure 12). A perceiver associates the product with a group of products such as a coffee maker. If the product's self-explanation is missing, a person will not be able to recognize the group of coffee makers to which the product belongs. In addition, self-explanation includes 'symbolic representation' (symbolische Aussage) (2b in figure 12), which provides information about other qualities associated with the product. For example, a kidney-shaped table can be related to products of the 1950s and to the atmosphere at that time. A showy car may impress passers-by and stop them or it may simply look ridiculous. The symbols are associated with things in the imagination, not only with the product at hand. The symbols (2b in figure 12) refer to cultural, historical and social features (Gros 1983, p.65–70).

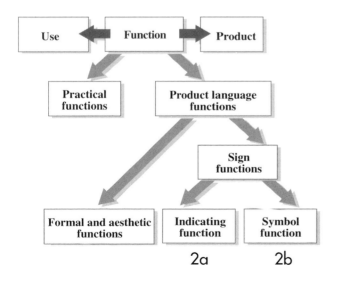

Figure 12. Signs and symbols (Gros 1983, p.70). I have numbered the sign function (Anzeichenfunktion) 2a and the symbolic function (Symbolfunktion) 2b to clarify the theory.

39

The sign of product language refers to the functions of the product (2a), and it has symbolic representation (2b). Gros compares this division with the division of a newspaper into a news section (2a) and a commentary section (2b). The news may be true or false. The commentaries, in turn, depend on points of view and are interpretations of the event. With respect to design products, one can say that news were important earlier but nowadays the commentaries take precedence.

Uri Friedländer (1984, p.14–15) used metaphors derived from nature, history, technology and the like in his applications of product semantics, which he calls 'metaphorical design'. For example, two different kinds of metaphorical languages can be seen in the front panel designs of two stereo amplifiers. The first uses a technical metaphor. The ribs are designed to refer to a heat sink, a symbol for power generation. The second uses a metaphor represented by a pyramid's enigmatic shape and expresses the magic of electronics.

Hans-Jürgen and Helga Lannoch (1984, 1987, 1989) have proposed an approach to design semantics by connecting it closer to the meanings of words in verbal language. They criticized current design language, which uses geometric terms, because the semantic dimension of a product is then neglected. In place of a geometric concept of the product form, the Lannochs introduced a form language which specifies the semantic space of a product. By using descriptive words like edgy, rough, open, low, sidewise, fastened, movable, and cosy the product's position and relations to the environment can be characterized along with its functions, usage and general impression. Using descriptive words, a designer can try to clarify the question of whether the product confirms the user's expectations or is misleading.

The analysis can be applied to design practice by relating descriptive words and the features of the product to each other. By analysing the meanings of words, a designer can construct a corresponding expression of form. The analysis will then serve design in forming visual expression with the help of words. Meaning is transferred from one medium to another, from verbal language to a product form. This 'semantic transfer' can be used in the beginning of the design process when functional and technical limitations are not yet under consideration. The analysis is a kind of form-finding process.

According to the Lannochs, a certain word does not unambiguously correspond to a certain visual form. There is no one-to-one relationship. The aim is to lessen technical domination in design, not to construct semantic iconography.

Communication as a problem

Product semantics, as developed by Klaus Krippendorff and Reinhart Butter (1984) dismisses the 'traditional semiotic sign' conceived as a triadic relationship (figure 13).

In figure 13 the sign and referent become one. The reference relation almost disappears, but the interpretation remains. The object refers to itself and to the whole of which it is a part. The interpretative relation, however, remains when, for example, a push button may suggest 'push me'. The links between the object and its user form a circle (figure 14). In this circular process the user manipulates the object and receives feedback through the consequences of actions, which lead to further manipulations and so forth.

According to this approach, the object is what it tells the user it is. But the form of the product may

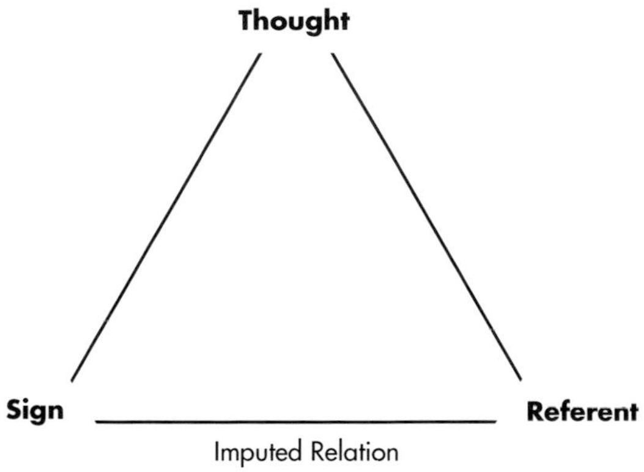

Figure 13. The object relation shrinks in the semiotic triangle constructed by Ogden and Richards in 1923, according to Krippendorff and Butter (1984, p.4).

41

product

user

Figure 14. The circular interaction between a user and a product.

be a problem of communication. A product disconnected from its context does not tell anything. Therefore, emphasis is placed on the social meanings and symbolic context of use. A product cannot be understood unless all its psychological and social contexts are known. According to Krippendorff and Butter product semantics requires that all possible connections be taken into account. In this respect, the theory becomes stale because such a requirement is too vast to be practical. The theory no longer structures semantic features of the design product.

Krippendorff and Butter (1984, p.8) aimed at offering designers a better means with which to analyse and improve the 'symbolic qualities' of form. This approach promises a better awareness of the symbolic processes underlying design. The concept 'symbolic quality' is, however, used without explicit meaning, and therefore the approach is weakened especially since the 'symbolic' is a much used term in many fields of knowledge and contexts. There is a vast amount of literature on symbols and the symbolic, as, for example, Goodman (1976), which Krippendorff does not refer to.

Since the concepts used by Krippendorff seem to be ambiguous and broad in their meanings, and since they have not been explicated, they can be misused, and a designer may be misled. Krippendorff warned many times of this possibility (1984, p.5 and 7; 1989, p.16). Because of its loosness, his approach to product semantics can be linked closely to marketing, which was not his purpose in the beginning. Sales are not a priority in design thinking. The improvement of product communication and the symbolic qualities of form are. People should be able to understand how products function and be able to manipulate them successfully.

42

The aim of Krippendorff's product semantics, as well as Gros' theory of product language, is to improve product design to facilitate communication between the product and its user. Alongside the traditional material and technical aspects of design, a communicative (or semantic) aspect is raised. The problem to be solved in design is transferred to the semantic dimension. In design, there is then an emphasis on the expressive skills and abilities of the designer as well. But this circumstance does not necessarily mean selfish design. By watching people's behaviour, designers may identify with the users or user groups and, in a way, design for themselves by taking the users' standpoint.

Sibylle Kicherer (1987) has studied industrial design from the viewpoint of a company. In her resourceful thesis, design has been conceived as communication. She analyses design in the light of research by Umberto Eco, Horst Oehlke and Jochen Gros. As a sign a product refers to (denotes) its visual image (Erscheinungsbild). Similarly the product denotes through its own features and functions. It refers always in a third way as well (connotation) and is determined by culture (i.e., a cultural code). Kicherer illustrates this phenomenon with the familiar example of the car as an indicator of social status. However, she does not examine the semiotic sign or the constitution of the sign any further. The thesis by Klöcker (1980), already dealt with in a preceding section, is interesting from the design point of view because it includes an analysis of concrete products. Penny Sparke (1987) has illustrated her broad surveys on design in cultural contexts with concrete examples. Her writing is product-centered and includes a great number of design products from various times and countries. Still, one can follow product variation only on a general level. Brigitte Wolf's thesis (1983) includes an analysis of vacuum cleaners. Her study is, however, mostly technical testing, and analyses the comfort of use. It relates to design only from these points of view. The theses by Horst Oehlke (1982) and Sibylle Kicherer (1987) do not include concrete applications or product examples of their own.

4. SEMIOTICS OF DESIGN PRODUCTS

A semantic analysis of a design product requires knowledge about the interpreter of the product (the human being), as well as about the product itself. Earlier studies have shown that the relationship between a product and its perceiver is complex. Therefore the approach chosen for this study must be specified. I would like to start by illustrating the perception process (figure 15).

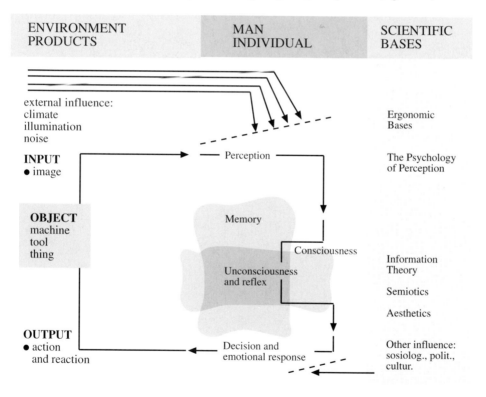

ENVIRONMENT PRODUCTS	MAN INDIVIDUAL	SCIENTIFIC BASES

external influence:
climate
illumination
noise

INPUT
● image

OBJECT
machine
tool
thing

Perception

Memory

Consciousness

Unconsciousness
and reflex

OUTPUT
● action
and reaction

Decision and
emotional response

Ergonomic
Bases

The Psychology
of Perception

Information
Theory

Semiotics

Aesthetics

Other influence:
sosiolog., polit.,
cultur.

Figure 15. The human being, the interaction with a product in the perception process, and a list of disciplines producing knowledge needed for the analysis of this interaction. The figure has been slightly modified from Klöcker (1980, p.34).

Figure 15 is a simplified illustration of the human perception process. It shows the environment including a product represented by a square. It includes the perceiving subject and a list of disciplines through which knowledge about the relationship is produced. The figure aims at illustrating a situation in which someone is perceiving a concrete product. The perception process proceeds in the direction shown in the figure from stimuli and sense impression of the product, both of which cause reactions and actions on the part of the perceiver. From figure 15, one might conclude that my analysis will concern a product subjectively perceived apart from its physical qualities. However, my aim is to analyse especially the product's features in this interactive process and not the human perceptual process as such.

Perception, learning and memory have been described as phases of one and the same process (Niiniluoto 1980, p.142; Nummenmaa et al. 1982, p.13; Arnheim 1974, p.45). Information grasped by the sense organs passes through many stages and is transformed already by the receptors on its way to the brain. According to James J. Gibson (1976, p.398) perception is an active process even before sensations have been aroused by stimuli. A perceiver is not fixed to a point; rather perception seems sequential. Information is extracted as one picks up invariants over time. The basic component of the percept is not a static image. Abraham Moles (1968, p.57) used the term 'scanning' when he, as did Gibson, emphasized activity as a basic quality of perception.

Human motives and attitudes influence the perception process. The emergence of motives is part of the development from childhood to adultness, and it is closely interconnected to cognitive development. The process results in various cognitive and motivational structures such as beliefs, attitudes and values, which differ in their generality, flexibility and level (Nummenmaa et al. 1982, p.19). The perception process is connected to broader social and cultural features (as indicated in figure 15). The physical environment influences the perception process as well (e.g., illumination, noise and climate).

The perception process can be studied by means of physiology. Impressions and subjective experiences are studied by psychology. In psychological studies the child's perception is conceived to be direct at first. Abstract concepts are then added at a later stage to the perception process. As the child grows older, the central nervous system adds more abstract and further processed qualities with the aid of thought processes. In learning a language, thinking is disconnected from the earlier direct perception, and the conceptual structuring of percepts becomes possible (Nummenmaa et al. 1982, p.52, 69 and 105).

However, the perception process has been described in another way in other psychological studies. Accordingly, direct perception and conceptual thinking are not separated. Or, at least, they are not phases following one another in a linear process. (See e.g. Gibson 1970, p.86; Arnheim 1974, p.46; and in connection with epistemology see Niiniluoto 1980, p.140–142.)

According to Arnheim (1974, p.45), people do not conceive perception as a process, which starts as singular elements are picked up and recorded. Vision does not seem to proceed from the particular to the general. On the contrary, overall structural features are primary in perception. For example, triangularity is not a late product of intellectual abstraction, but a direct and more fundamental experience than a singular detail of the figure. Young children see 'doggishness' before they are able to distinguish one dog from another.

Perception can be conceived as an active and even a creative process. But all information-based perception that regulates human action is not conscious. Perception is also habitual and instinctive.

Information in perception

Information is mediated in the perception process. There are two kinds of information, physical and semantic, of which the latter concerns expression and use of human language (Niiniluoto 1989, p.48). According to Gibson (1976, p.397), perception is information-based, not sensation-based. The content of information can, for many reasons, be erroneous or wrong (misperceptions, illusions), and it may involve false existential assumptions (Niiniluoto 1980, p.142).

Knowledge about the world directs people's perception processes and affects expectations. Positive feed back, which corresponds to expectations, will encourage people to continue, and strengthen their actions. Readiness to act is inseparable from experiences. Inherited abilities conceived as contrasting with learned capabilities is a misleading idea (Nummenmaa et al. 1982, p.14–17 and 128). The significance of preconceptions can even be seen in everyday experience because perceptions are active interpretations. In Edmund Husserl's philosophy, it is called the intentionality of perception, and Ludwig Wittgenstein refers to it with 'seeing as' (Niiniluoto 1980, p.224).

What is seen?

The term 'seeing as' is similar to Gibson's psychological concept 'perceive affordance'. Things have perceivable qualities, which can be called affordances. They afford themselves to something when they are perceived. For example a product can afford sitting. It is seen as something which one can sit on. The perception of the product is connected with the perception of its function. Gibson (1976, p.404–405) noted that not only things, but also matter, places, events and animals afford something. He has listed different examples of affordances.

A product can afford lifting, throwing, turning and the like. Kurt Koffka used the term 'demand character' for this feature in his research in the 1930s. For example, a post box invites the posting of a letter; a handle wants to be grasped. Things tell people what to do with them. Koffka assumed this demand character to be in the percept, not in the physical object. Martin Krampen (1989, p.126) uses the term 'invitation character'. (The German word is 'Aufforderungscharakter', introduced earlier by Kurt Lewin.)

Gibson (1976, p.409), in contrast, conceives affordance as a quality of the object in relation to its perceiver. The layout (of the surfaces) of the object is visible and determines its use. Affordance does not change if the need of the perceiver changes. The walk-on ability of a surface exists whether or not it is walked on. It offers what it does because it is what it is.

Hans-Jürgen Lannoch's view is close to Gibson's. In his theoretical approach to product semantics, Lannoch uses the term 'action opportunity' (in German Handlungsmöglichkeit, 1987, p.13), which is a (perceivable) feature of a product.

Affordance was restricted in the preceding discussion to the perception of products and their possible functions and qualities. Gibson widened this concept. In psychology perception of meaning is also spoken of. Gibson defined affordance as the perception of meaning by combining the function and meaning of a product. Accordingly, the meaning of a product would be what the product affords.

Affordance has two directions. First, it stretches to the product's physical existence through its form, size, and composition. Second, these define the thing, what it affords, and its meaning. The perception of a product cannot be separated from the perception of its meaning. When people see the length and solidity of a surface, they also see that they can walk on it. Therefore, it can no longer be assumed that there is first a sense impression, after which a meaning is added to it. (Compare to the preceding discussion of Arnheim's views.) Perceptions are connected very closely to specific things as Martin Heidegger (1977, p.10) pointed out. In his view things are even closer to us than all our impressions of them. Accordingly, someone hears the three-motored plane, the Mercedes in immediate distinction from the Adler, the door shut in the house instead of tones, noises and voices as acoustic sense impressions in general.

The theory of perception by Gibson has been popular among design theoreticians in writings about design education and design products (Kepes 1966; Smets 1987; Krippendorff 1989; Krampen 1989; Bush 1990). An interesting aspect from the point of view of this study is that Gibson's affordance depends on the product's form and on the features of its shape. Accordingly, the product's form is especially important in the analysis of its meaning because people see the product's affordance in seeing its form (Gibson 1951, p.303–316).

A study of visual composition and principles belongs traditionally to the education of a designer. Knowledge about the psychology of perception has been applied to student's exercises. This knowledge concerns two- and three-dimensional forms, open and closed forms, static and dynamic forms, the visual weight of a form, impressions of the depth of a surface, effects of contrast in light and colour, and the like. Pedagogical basic courses have been planned that advance systematically from simple two-dimensional sketches towards more complex three-dimensional experiments (Wingler 1980; Kepes 1959; Zitzmann 1984, 1986 and 1987). Gibson (1976, p.416) criticized basic courses in the education of architects and product designers because they almost neglect the composition of three-dimensional forms, which are even more essential to design thinking than two-dimensional forms are. Gibson stressed the difference between the perception of three-dimensional form and the perception of pictures. (See also Akner Koler 1992.) When people move around in the environment, they do not perceive colour and form as such on surfaces; instead they perceive the affordance of various surfaces and lay-outs of surfaces in space. People modify the products of their environment according to the affordance of the products, and not according to forms and colours as such. People do not perceive good form, abstract form, mathematically elegant form as such in their everyday environments. What is seen is rather different opportunities to act, such as walking, sitting, resting, climbing, moving, using, hiding, taking and eating. Gibson notes one especially important mode of affordance of a surface, namely, the perception of a corner, which enables us to move behind it. The perceiver sees a hidden surface behind the corner. Architects and designers should keep people's movements and actions in mind.

Dimensions of a product

Aristotle distinguished four different bases for understanding something. A product can be explained by its material, structure, efficient cause and purpose. The scholastics used the terms material cause, formal cause, effective cause and final cause for a similar concept of understanding (Niiniluoto 1983, p.236–237). These four explanatory aspects are close to the four semiotic dimensions Max Bense (1971, p.78–82) introduced for a design product. The product can be divided into the following four different dimensions: the material dimension (hyletics), the dimension of technique and construction (syntax), the dimension of technical product form (semantics), and the dimension of use (pragmatics). (See figure 6, p.24.)

The pragmatic dimension in figure 6 is a circle around the other three dimensions. The product's functions in use cannot be explained on the basis of its technical properties only. One cannot understand the pragmatics of a product if all of its dimensions are not considered. The pragmatic dimension is conceived as resulting from the other three. The line is broken between the material and technical dimension; and this break only indicates that one cannot speak of a product on the basis of material only, before something has been constructed or made out of a material. The broken line indicates the wholeness in principle. There is then a circle, a whole, where the syntax is based on the material.

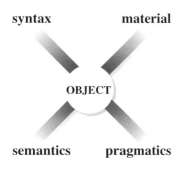

Figure 16. The four dimensions of a design product (modified from Bense 1971).

I have slightly modified Bense's figure for the purpose of my analysis. (See figure 16.) The figure is a simplified illustration of a design product and seems to offer a versatile approach. Therefore, it seems useful and stimulating for the analysis. This concept illuminates various aspects of the thing, but remains a whole, and prevents a thing from falling apart.

Martin Heidegger (1977, p.11–13), in his philosophical discussion on the thingly of a thing, conceives matter (hyle) and form (morphe) as constant in a thing. The thing solicits us by its outer appearance (eidos). This conception is close to my figure in which the thing is formed matter. A jug, an ax, a shoe are also matter occurring in form. The interfusion of form and matter is controlled by the purposes of these products. Usefulness of, for example, a jug is not something added afterwards, nor is it something that floats somehow on top of it as an end. Usefulness is a basic feature, in which both the formative act and the choice of material are grounded. In this respect the pragmatic dimension differs from Bense's formulation, where the circle was conceived as a resulting total dimension. Usefulness as a basic feature seems more appropriate from the design point of view, because the design product is intended to serve a practical purpose.

The material dimension includes the product's material. But, in this study, I consider material properties only when they are connected with the other dimensions because my research is not about the chemical composition, durability or other similar characteristics of the material. I, therefore, simply briefly consider material aspects, being well aware of the fact that the materials chosen for a certain product influence the other dimensions.

The syntactic dimension covers the product's structure and technical functioning. The structure consists of parts and the way they are connected to each other. With respect to the pragmatic Bensenian total dimension, the product is examined in use. In the following discussion, I apply the concept presented in figure 16 to a design product. I begin with the syntactic dimension.

The syntactic dimension

The syntax of a product can be illustrated by technical drawings, breakdowns and mock-ups. The syntactic dimension includes both the analysis of the product's technical construction and an analysis of visual details such as joints, openings, holes, form crossings, texture, graphics and colours.

These details can also be described as features of visual composition, such as simplicity and complexity of the overall form, symmetry, balance, dynamics and rhythm. Klöcker (1980, p.85) called such features 'mathematical qualities of form'. He distinguished between the arithmetic, geometric and topological qualities of form. Rhythm, for example, is an arithmetic quality and a very effective and useful tool in visual composition. Rhythm requires repetition of visual detail (a line, a figure) in the form. It can be, for example, regular or freely flowing, tramping, smooth or fragmentary. (See, e.g., Itten 1975, p.98.) One detail can not only influence another visual component but also the overall form as well. Similarly one colour affects another colour in a composition. Colour also affects the visual impression of size and the dynamics of form.

The relationship between the technical construction of the product and the environment should be recognized. A product may be distinct or it may assimilate into its surroundings. The relationship can be neutral or dominated by either the product or the environment into which the product may merge. A product form may be coherent, divergent or ambiguous (Klöcker 1980, p.98). Many domestic appliances, for example, have been designed to be neutral and assimilate into a kitchen environment. The visual structure of a product can be described verbally with adjectives and other figures of speech, for example, as Lannoch (1987, p.12) suggested in his 'semantic transfer'. He conceived adjectives and figures of speech as expressing semantic qualities, except for 'geometric' words like spherical, square, and so forth.

The syntactic dimension can be hidden in a box or put under a cover. Then it is mediated to the perceiver only through a manual or a picture. A hidden syntax can be illustrated in an assembly drawing, but then a person cannot see all of the syntactic features (e.g., movements) (figure 17).

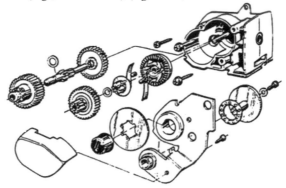

Figure 17. The syntax of a product in an assembly drawing.

The pragmatic dimension

The pragmatic dimension of a product is analysed from the point of view of its use, for example, from an ergonomic or sociological point of view (who uses the product, in what kind of situation is the product used). In a wide sense, the pragmatic dimension includes the whole 'life cycle' of the product, from a designer's drawing board to the dump. (See also figure 9.)

Paulsson and Paulsson (1956) have analysed different kinds of 'uses' of design products. Their 'use' includes the product's practical, social and aesthetic use. An analysis, for example, of domestic knives like a bread knife, a fruit knife, or a meat knife, would not be sensible without knowledge of their pragmatics. In the same way, the knives of a butcher or a fisherman would have strange descriptions if they have not been considered in the context of their use, which would reveal the main purpose of the knives. The material of a sailor's knife handle is cork in order to prevent the knife from sinking. The choice of the handle material is caused by conditions of use and is not merely due to the requirements of a grip in cutting.

53

It can be concluded that the Paulssons conceived a product's 'use' very widely when they labelled social and aesthetic aspects as 'uses' as well. For example, a telephone would be designed to look like a fairy-tale figure because of a 'use'. The product would have a 'use' as a telecommunication instrument on one hand and as a toy on the other. Playing and joking are both included in the 'use' of this telephone. Evidently products can have many kinds of usage in various situations, but it seems tricky to explain the form of the product from such a broad point of view of 'use'.

When knowledge about the product's material, construction and technical function (syntax) is added to a wide conception of 'use', there seems to be a sufficient number of bases for my analysis. Three kinds of causes have emerged: the material, the formal (technical) and the use. The beginning seems good. But the problem for further analysis is precisely here, in the broad concept of 'use'. 'Use' is conceived as too loose and roomy, and, therefore, further analysis is blocked.

Therefore the concept of 'use' must be defined anew. In this study, I have considered 'use' as the practical use of the product. Then at least, 'aesthetic use' remains outside the definition. I have, however, widened the pragmatics in another direction to embrace the product's whole existence, from its planning to its destruction (or recycling), as illustrated in figure 9. The pragmatic dimension of a product includes knowledge about the users and about the ecological impact and economic effects on business and production. As has already been noted, a product can have many tasks and purposes. This multiplicity does not prevent a person from defining the main task for which a tool has been designed, however. And, connecting the analysis of a product to one main purpose of use does not prevent a person from seeing other uses for the same product.

When the whole life cycle is included in the pragmatics of a product, knowledge is also included about its designer, manufacturer, marketing, sales, buyers, consumption, consumer tests, legislation, and history. (See also Schürer 1969; Kicherer 1987.)

Sigfried Giedion (1948) studied design products from a cultural history point of view. His work is an example of a pragmatic approach. Giedion's study also covers other aspects of design products, namely, materials, techniques and meaning. It is stimulating with the respect to design analysis because Giedion used concrete examples to illustrate people's attitudes towards new products. He connected concrete examples to the main theme of his work: the mechanization of work and production.

As has already been seen, a product such as a telephone may not be determined by technical or even ergonomic aspects alone, neither by its practical function nor by the environment, but by a fairy-tale figure. It now seems obvious that the pragmatic dimension (with the help of material and syntax) will not be sufficient for a description and explanation of a design product.

The semantics of a product

When the literature on design is examined, product semantics seems to be an incoherent and broad dimension. In the beginning of this chapter, I noted that the semantic dimension of a thing corresponds to the 'purpose' of the product and to its 'final cause'. The purpose of a design product is mainly practical, and I included it in the pragmatic dimension in the previous section. It seems that use, purpose and form are closely entwined. The pragmatic and semantic aspects seem to merge.

If a product is considered to have only three dimensions (material, syntax, and pragmatics), the fourth would have to be left out, and thereby semantics would be neglected. In other words, one of the possible dimensions would remain untreated. Obviously, a design product includes a pragmatic purpose since it serves a practical task. For example, the purpose of a chair is to function as equipment for sitting. The 'use' (sitting) would be the same as the 'purpose' (sitting). Pragmatics would be the same as semantics. Therefore, semantics cannot be analysed from the point view of 'purpose'. Another way must be found. The questions must be presented in a new way so that something, which could be called the semantic dimension, can be delineated.

What does the product represent?

How is the purpose of a product expressed or presented?

In what kind of environment does a product seem to belong?

The expressive and representational qualities of a product may be central aspects of the semantic dimension. The semantic dimension adds representational aspects (i.e., the references) to the syntax (Niiniluoto 1989, p.25). For example, a chair affords its purpose of use and, at the same time, a way of sitting. The questions in the semantic dimension are, how does the chair afford sitting, and how does the chair express the possibility of sitting and what else does it express. The representational qualities of a café chair, a garden chair and an office chair are different. The cause is not only a pragmatic and material one, but also a matter of representation.

The semantics of a product may change if the material is changed. For example, the same jug form can be made in porcelain and in stoneware (Paulsson and Paulsson 1965, p. 59–61). The practical function of the jug is the same in both cases, but the jugness is not the same because the jugs are made of different materials and have different ways of expressing jugness.

In the following discussion, I introduce topics such as product identity, ideal type, model, adaptation to the environment, gifts and souvenirs that may contribute to a semantic analysis. They have also been dealt with in earlier design studies. These issues cannot be analysed free of the other dimensions. In fact, they are simply qualities that can be characterized as semantic.

Product identity

Klöcker (1980, p.225–232) applied Ellinger's information theory to describe the identity of a design product. According to the theory, the better the product informs, the stronger its identity. Identity can be approached from the following three kinds of information:

1. Information about existence: being existent as a material object, the product expresses (announces) 'here is a thing'.
2. Information about origin: the product informs about its designer, manufacturer, country and culture.
3. Information about quality: the product informs about its function, use and maintenance.

Ideal type

One way of describing a design product from a semantic point of view is to form its ideal type (i.e., a semantic type), which cannot be reduced solely to its construction and technique. Neither is the ideal type a sum of its practical functions. For example, the ideal type of a jug can be characterized on the basis of jugness. The more jugness it has, the closer it is to an ideal jug type. Similarly the radio-like features of a radio or the home-like qualities of a home can be characterized. Uday Athavankar (1990) has argued for the categorization of designed products on the basis of defined ideal types. He referred to the experiments of Eleanor Rosch (1975), in which she found that people classify things according to 'natural categories'. An ideal type represents the characteristic features of a product group (cups, jugs, radios). The ideal type can be an established form, such as the electric bulb. A detail of a product can also become an ideal type. An ideal type can be described with adjectives such as fast (car) and warm (coat). The typical character of the type is then the speed (of the car) and the warming (of the coat).

A slower car is further away from the ideal type of a car and less car-like; a less warming coat is further away from the ideal type of a coat and is less coat-like.

A product can refer to an ideal type and, at the same time, have a specific reference to another realm. For example, a baby shoe may refer to shoeness (i.e., the ideal type of shoes) and, at the same time, refer to babyness. A high-tech watch may refer to clockness and, at the same time, to a highly developed and complex technique in which mechanisms and many tiny details are apparent and which is appreciated by experts.

The ideal type may be associated with the ideas of the Purists in the 1920s. The Purists thought that a few basic forms could be derived in the analysis of all products. Thus all forms could be optimized (Steadman 1979, p.145). In the following discussion, I use the term 'characteristic form' instead of 'ideal type' so that my intention will not be confused with the Purists' ideas, but instead relates to typical features of a product group as explicated by Rosch (1975).

Model

In addition to its practical functioning, a design product is apparent, exhibited and on display. In this sense, the product may refer to exemplary products used by historical persons and celebrities. Exemplaries like this may even form a style. Through the style, the products are associated with persons and milieus and life styles (e.g., Louis XVI). The product forms of the exemplaries are transferred (within the style) to other products and users and widen their field of application. The style of the exemplaries may even be seen in everyday things and mass-produced objects. Big, technically new and complex products like space ships and racing cars are used as master products and influence the design of smaller and more common products. Master products function as formal and aesthetic models. Their style is transferred. With models a product may follow fashion trends (Dorfles 1966, Schürer 1969, Oehlke 1982). The exemplary thing impresses because people want to identify themselves with a current positive development.

Adaptation to the environment

When the surroundings change, a product in these surroundings may change as well – and in the same direction. When, for example, a kitchen is transformed into a more spacious and less loading work environment, all its fixtures are adjusted to this change. Different kitchen utensils such as the stove, refrigerator, cabinets, washbasin and dishwasher are designed in accordance with the overall aim and the standardized kitchen (Schürer 1969, p.20).

The chair changes when it is moved from the kitchen to the living room. As opposed to the kitchen chair, the living room chair is not mainly used for sitting, but is meant for relaxing, being on display and exemplifying the interior decoration of the room (Paulsson and Paulsson 1956, p.69). The different forms of an evening bag and a shopping bag do not depend only on their practical uses either. The Paulssons have pointed out that the environment, places (rooms), occasions and the like in which products are used influence the design of the product as well. Especially in social situations, people are required to have specific attitudes or feelings and to behave accordingly. The products used are adjusted accordingly. They are in 'social use'. A person must know the rules of the game to be able to choose the right product. Even the products belong to the game. Accordingly products have symbolic meaning based on conventional habits and patterns of habits. A chair may have an overdose of symbolic meaning as, for example, a throne or a chairperson's chair emphasized by its placement in the room. A throne with animal forms in its detail was, in the past, thought to transfer magic power. (See also Eco 1968, p.24.)

The power was thought to be transmitted through the forms to the person seated on the throne. Even nowadays products with similar details exist, but they have lost their original symbolic meaning. As motifs of form they are, however, still used. They are conceived as mere decorations or they have been given new meanings. A chair that mainly functions in a social context is often designed with a rich and expressive form. It may have 'more form' than necessary for the purpose of sitting. The freedom of form may seem unlimited. A similarly functioning example is the chairperson's gavel. The form of the gavel is almost indifferent from a practical point of view. Its main purpose is to refer to the chairperson, his or her position in the group, the members, tradition and activities of the society (Paulsson and Paulsson 1956, p.75). Common everyday products can function as symbols, too. They can have a historical or literal connection that requires background knowledge and learning.

Gifts and souvenirs

Gifts and souvenirs are typical products whose practical function is of secondary importance (at least at the moment of giving and remembering). For example, souvenirs often have an emphasized symbolic meaning, as in the sense described by the Paulssons.

The practical function (and related technical function) can be hidden. A thing may look like the Eiffel Tower and refer to memories of Paris and, at the same time, it may hide a mechanism (e.g., a pencil sharpener). The secondary role of the practical task may explain the often weak material and technical functioning of souvenirs.

Products as signs

As I have already stated, I wish to examine a product's representational qualities on the semantic dimension and try to answer what a thing may represent and how it expresses something about itself (its use, purpose of use) and about something else. The way in which the purpose of a product, for example, a chair, appears cannot be the product's intrinsic quality only. Neither is it in the users' minds when they look at the thing. A semantic quality should, therefore, be looked upon as a relationship between the product, its representation and its user.

In order to develop further the analysis of this relationship, I would like to apply a semiotic approach. In Charles S. Peirce's philosophy of signs, the semiotic sign is triadic. 'A sign or representamen, is something which stands to somebody for something in some respect or capacity' (*CP* 2.228). (References to Peirce are to volumes and paragraphs, not to pages, of the Collected Papers.) Accordingly, the relation between a perceivable thing, its representation and an interpreting subject is called a sign. A design product can also be considered a sign. Then the product has the characteristics of a semiotic sign. The sign is conceived as anything that functions in a triadic relation:

$$z=R(M,O,I),$$

where z = the sign, R = relation, M = medium or representamen, O = object and I = interpretant. The sign is not an object, but a relation. The sign z is a triadic relation in which something in some respect or capacity (M) refers to something (O), which means something when somebody interprets it (I) (figure 18).

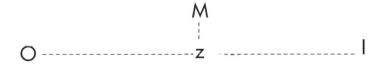

Figure 18. Peirce's triadic sign, as illustrated by Bense (1971, p.102).

The three parts of the sign form the object relation (M–O) and the interpretant relation (M-I). The sign functions at the same time as a transmitter, an indicator and a meaning (als Vermittlung, Bezeichnung und Bedeutung). The object relation is its indicator and the interpretant relation is its meaning (*CP* 1.339; also Bense 1971, p.27).

Depending on the viewpoint, products can function as signs or signs can be produced with the help of products (Eco 1979, p.48 and 151). The sign function of a product requires intellectual productive labour and learning and cannot be understood as a mere reception of and reaction to stimuli. The interpretation of signs is an interactive sign process, semiosis.

The meanings of products as signs can be analysed by dividing their references into two parts, primary references and secondary references. Eco (1968, p.20–23) has illustrated this possibility with the example of a building. A building refers primarily to a form of inhabitation, which is its denotative reference. It also refers more widely to a certain conception of inhabitation, an overall ideology of inhabitation and use, which has influenced its design and which is called its connotative reference. Arches of various forms, for example, denote their load-bearing function, 'but they connote diverse ways of conceiving the function: they begin to assume a symbolic function' (Eco 1968, p.21). In the analysis of cultural things such as buildings and other design products Eco has distinguished between the signification and communication of a thing. The study of signification is a prerequisite for the study of communication.

The application of a sign to a concrete product seems complicated. (See, e.g., Eco 1972, p.229.) In design literature (Klöcker 1980, Oehlke 1982 and 1988, Bürdek 1991), sign functions are not made explicit. One is not told how a product actually functions as a sign and how the sign is applicable in order to improve an analysis of a design product. It has hitherto been sufficient merely to mention that the product functions as a sign, but no description is given of how this happens. Therefore, the sign has remained abstract as a label on a book's page without content. The sign has not been useful either for analysis in design studies or for design practice. In spite of good intentions to examine the semantic aspect of a product, this attempt has usually stopped here.

The seemingly complicated semiotic sign is even considered useless without any explicit arguments about its unsuitability. Those who do not consider the sign or have rejected the sign (Kinross 1986, Krippendorff 1989) have explained their rejection rather than analysed the sign. Since they did not discuss the sign, it remains unclear how they in fact conceived it. One erroneous conception about the application is the fact that signs are considered to be similar to words or sentences in verbal language.

In the following discussion, I attempt to show how signs are applicable so that their function can be understood and they can possibly be used for design purposes.

Eco (1979, p.23) has illustrated the constitution of semiosis as a cultural phenomenon. He gives an example of a primitive man, the Australopithecus, and two stones (S1 and S2). This man finds a stone (S1) and uses it. Eco notes that the semiotic process begins when the man finds another stone (S2), which he recognizes can perform the same task as the first stone (S1). S2 may function in the same way as S1, which the man found earlier.

Figure 19 illustrates a semiotic process in which the user of stones (the primitive man) has conceived the stones as belonging to the same type (St) and he does not look at them merely as separate entities. 'Encountering S2 and being able to subsume it under type St, our Australopithecus regards it as the sign-vehicle of a possible function' (Eco 1979, p.23). The type St, which has now been constituted, refers to the same task or function (F) as the two stones. Stones S1 and S2 have a significant form because they refer to a function (F), which the primitive man in Eco's example conceived. It can be said that both the two stones and the object type have significant forms.

The possibility to give a name to type St adds a new dimension to the beginning of a semiotic process (figure 19). The name denotes the type St and connotes the possible function F of the type (and the objects) at the same time. Eco's illustration is close to a situation in which a product is conceived as a sign. Type St refers to a function and can be given a name. A situation appears, in which the name and its references (the reference of a word) can be analysed rather than the product and its references being examined. The material sign vehicles (the two stones) in Eco's illustration provide a good starting point for the application of the semiotic sign.

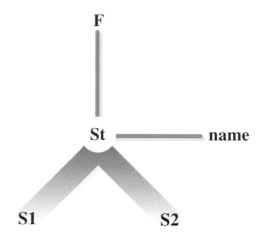

Figure 19. The beginning of semiosis according to Eco.

Bense's and Eco's approaches both include material sign vehicles that are outside the triadic sign relation (like stones S1 and S2 in figure 19).

The constitution of the sign according to Peirce

I would now like to turn the triangle in figure 19 and give the apices new names, Eco's figure therefore being altered slightly. I would like to apply the triadic relation in a Peircean way, widen the content of the apices and give them terms used by Peirce. The type St (the significant form) then becomes the representamen R, the relationship to its function (St–F) is the object relation (R–O), and the naming of the relation (St–name) is the interpretant relation (R–I) (figure 20).

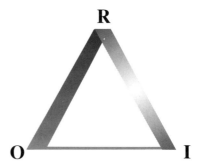

Figure 20. The semiotic sign.

Just changing the names in a figure will obviously not suffice. I have to explain the meaning and content of the different parts of the triad. Such triangles are familiar from philosophical and semiotic literature, but they have been difficult to apply in design analyses because they have not been explicated. Perhaps it has been unclear what representamen R actually means and how it differs from its referent, the object O. Both figures 18 and 20 simply illustrate a sign as a triadic whole in the sense of Peirce.

Signs are divisible by three tricothomies (*CP* 2.243): first, according to the sign itself; second, according to the relation to its object; third, according to its interpretant, that is first according to the representamen R, second, according to R–O, and third, according to R–I.

The means for interpretation: R

When a product is perceived it represents and expresses something to the one who interprets it. What is then perceived? When, in my study, I especially consider visual perception the answer would be 'form'. It is the form that represents something interpreted. Accordingly, the perceived form is the representamen R as shown in figures 18 and 20. Form R functions as a medium in the interpretation (i.e., in the O–R–I relation). (See figure 20.) Form R is the means for interpretation. It refers in different modes to its object O. These references or object relations (R–O) are the focus of my analysis.

The 'form' of a design product has, then, a twofold meaning. On the syntactic level it is a technical construction and a visual composition. It has, accordingly, technical qualities and features of visual compositions. Within the semantic dimension 'form' is a means (representamen) for interpretation and refers to something.

The object O of the sign

Next, I examine what R refers to and how R refers to something. Therefore, it is time to take a closer look at the relation R–O. Figure 21 shows Peirce's three different modes of reference in the object relation R–O. The sign may refer as an icon, index and a symbol to its object O. O can be another thing, action, fact, event, quality or the like.

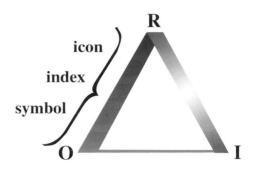

Figure 21. Three modes of reference of a semiotic sign.

Göran Sonesson (1989, p.203) uses the term 'referent' for the object O in the object relation of a sign. He uses the term 'expression' for R. In my opinion, the object relation of a sign can be shortened to 'reference' for the ease of style (although it still is always the relation R–O and part of the whole triad O–R–I). The replacement of the representamen with 'expression' is, however, misleading. Expression is an object relation, too. The terminology applied by Sonesson seems to confuse the different conceptions of the triadic and dyadic signs, and the terms of the triadic sign may easily intermingle with the terminology of the Saussurean dyadic sign. More problems can result, for example, when one considers Louis Hjelmslev's division of the dyadic sign into the form of expression and the content of expression on the signifier side of the dyadic sign.

The interpretant I

The interpretant is conceived as being like a process of interpretation, an on-going sign production. According to Peirce (*CP* 5.284), the interpretant is not equivalent to an individual interpreter. However, a triadic sign necessarily involves an interpreter (Niiniluoto 1986, s.44).

> A sign addresses somebody, that is, it creates in the mind of that person an equivalent sign, or perhaps a more developed sign. (*CP* 2.228)

A dyadic sign

The semiotic theory of Ferdinand de Saussure conceives a sign as a dyadic entity. This sign has two sides: the signifier (signifiant) and the signified (signifié), the sign-vehicle and the meaning (Eco 1979, p.14). It seems to me that the dyadic sign is not as suitable for an analysis of a design product as the triadic one because it emphasizes the signified side of the sign and gives the signifier less attention. Accordingly, it does not take the materiality of the product enough into consideration even though it has a signifier or expressive side. The interpretative side is thus emphasized and the analysis may loosen its grip on the material product. In my view, an analysis of a design product with the aid of Saussure's sign would easily depart from its object.

The triadic sign

The Peircean sign seems a more delicate approach to their analysis than the dyadic concept of the sign. With the triadic sign one is able to analyse the reference relations of the material product, its object relations (R–O). In the analysis, the material product can be conceived as a sign vehicle. Even though the material product is not placed in the apices of the triangle, neither in R nor in O, the analysis of the sign does not, according to Peirce, exclude the study of a physical thing.

> The mind is not a receptable, which if a thing is in, it ceases to be out of. (*CP* 8.16)

> It follows from our own existence that everything which is present to us is a phenomenal manifestation of ourselves. This does not prevent its being a phenomenon of something without us, just as a rainbow is at once a manifestation of both the sun and the rain. (*CP* 5.283)

The iconic sign

The iconic sign is a triadic sign that refers to an O 'merely by virtue of characters of its own, it is like that thing and used as a sign of it' (*CP* 2.247). Peirce calls the iconic sign a 'hypoicon' as well. There are three kinds of hypoicons: images, diagrams and metaphors (*CP* 2.276 and 2.277). When this mode of reference is applied in the analysis of a design product, the product functions as an iconic sign, and the form (R) is interpreted as being like something else, the form seems to resemble another form. Two forms are associated when their features are perceived to be similar.

For example, I may interpret a dredge as an iconic sign when I see it in action on an open lake. I may associate its features with the form of a water bird by means of similarity, and its movements may be similar to those of the bird as well. When I interpret the dredge as an iconic sign (the form of the dredge being similar to the form of the bird), I may recognize similarities to a bird (O). Such a perception produces an iconic sign. The iconic sign may be a sudden flash of recognition, but it may also emerge in contemplation more slowly.

A telephone may also function as an iconic sign when its handle refers to a human head, the position of the head and the expression of the head's position and further to the 'state of mind' in this head, its mood, sadness, pride, and the like. The form of the telephone (R) represents the 'other' form with the help of similar qualities.

The forms of products can often be seen as iconic signs when they are interpreted as forms of plants, animals, fairy-tale figures, comic figures, historical celebrities, events and the like. An iconic sign may represent an attitude, a mood or a feeling. Such expressiveness is often called product metaphor in design literature. (See, e.g., Krohn and McCoy 1989, p.118.)

Similarity only does not suffice as grounds for an iconic sign (Goodman 1976, p.77). A car, for example, cannot function as an iconic sign of another similar car. A blue Volkswagen cannot function as an iconic sign of another similar blue Volkswagen. The other blue Volkswagen is a double. A metaphoric reference also requires a shift in realm. The car functions as a metaphor when its form refers to a similar form in another realm such as to the form of an insect, for example, a beetle. Then the form of the beetle (O) is a metaphor of the form of the car (R).

The colour of a product may function as an iconic sign when it refers to another thing with similar colour. Gray may refer, for example, to concrete even though the material is not really concrete.

The index

The index is a sign that is affected by its object (*CP* 2.248). It is in a real and dynamic connection with its object (*CP* 2.287 and 2.305). The reference relation R–O actually exists. An index is contiguous to its object O. For example, smoke is an index of fire. An imprint of a foot in the sand can be an index of someone who walked on the beach. Traces of the product may refer to a tool used in a specific means of production. The traces indicate what kind of a tool caused them. Trace R refers to tool O.

An index may refer to a certain direction (a weathercock, a finger) and draw attention to that direction (*CP* 2.286). A handle may function as such an index as well. An index draws attention by being really existent and not by being similar, as the iconic sign does.

The symbol

The symbol is a conventional sign depending on habit: 'Etymologically, it should mean a thing thrown together ... the making of a contract or convention' (*CP* 2.297). A symbol refers through an association of general ideas, but it does not, in itself, identify the things (*CP* 2.249 and 2.298). It is thus itself a general type, and the object O to which it refers is also of a general nature. The symbol is connected with its object O by virtue of the idea of the symbol-using mind, without which no such connection would exist (*CP* 2.299). Through use and experience, its meaning grows (*CP* 2.302). A symbol acts through a Replica (*CP* 2.249; 2.292). For example, words, graphics and colours can function as symbolic signs. They are embodied by means of replicas. Symbolic signs can be forms of any kind because neither similarity to the object of reference nor a real connection is a basis for the interpretation. Symbolic signs are, however, not wholly arbitrary within a specific culture. They are instead based on established habits and forms. A balance is used to symbolize justice and it would be difficult to imagine, for example, a chariot in its place. (This is an example by Saussure in Lotman 1990, p.260.) Symbolic references must be known in order to be understood. Trademarks, names and numbers are common symbols in design products.

A product can express a quality like lightness, sorrow, energy, flexibility, cleanness and nobility. It does not, however, possess these qualities. A product is not necessarily speedy, even if it looks fast moving. Then the product refers metaphorically. It is conceived as having features similar to those of some experienced as fast. This reference is not a symbolic one. But it might become symbolic when the content of the reference has been agreed upon. For example, it can be agreed that a form is a symbol of lightness or speed, that a feather symbolizes lightness and a certain ball-like shape is a symbolic sign of wool (as a material).

The cultural and social background of the person who interprets a product also influences sign production. Accordingly, different persons may interpret the same product in a setting in various ways. For example, a metaphorical reference interpreted by someone may not be interesting from some other person's point of view. Nevertheless, metaphorical interpretation should not be prohibited in the design context in general. On the contrary, when the diverse backgrounds of personal interpretations are recognized, they enrich sign production.

Why is a metaphorical reference not only interesting but also useful in the design context? It seems to me that a metaphorical reference illuminates a specific characteristic of a product. This specific mode of reference can be seen as a means for creating images and optional images. Designers often speak of products as looking like something. In fact, the interpretation of metaphorical references is already part of a discursive practice rather than an alien element introduced by the semiotic approach in this study.

Misleading applications of the sign

It may be useful for my further study to discuss some possible misleading attempts at applying the sign to a design product. A vague and ambiguous application may block the analysis and lead to a dead end. In the first case, the material product is placed inside the triadic relation, as O in the object relation R–O (figure 22).

How then can the means of interpretation, the representamen R, be defined? R can be either a picture of the product or a name (a word) which refers to the product O, which is the material product itself. In this case, the product is no longer analysed as a sign because the representamen is a picture or a word. The representamen is no longer a means with which to interpret the product, but is its picture or name (a word). The analysis can now be focused on the references of a picture or a word, and this is the semiotics of

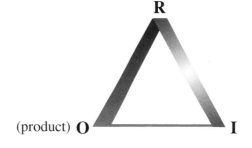

Figure 22. A triadic sign in which the design product is O.

pictures or words, but not the semiotics of design products. The analysis of the product does not advance.

In the second case, the design product (as a material object) is placed inside the triadic relation, both in the place of the object O and in the place of R (figure 23).

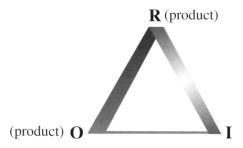

R (product)

(product) **O**   **I**

Figure 23. The design product is both the representamen R and its object O.

Now the product is a means (R) for interpretation and refers to itself (O). R and O merge. It follows that the triadic relation is transformed to a dyadic relation. Accordingly, there is the material design product (as both O and R) on one hand and its interpretation (I) on the other. The product and its interpretation by someone (R-I) remain. This process brings the study back to its beginning.

In my view, the product does not merely refer to itself, to its material and syntax only. In that case it would exclude all of the other kinds of possible references that have already been discussed. Instead, the question is whether the design product refers to itself at all or to something else? Or, does it refer to itself as a material object and, at the same time, to something else?

According to Barthes (1964), all products in a culture refer as signs to their uses. First, they present themselves as practical instruments, for example, the telephone as an instrument for verbal communication, the pencil as a tool for writing. Second, their practical function supports cultural meanings, which do not depend on actual usage. For example, a white telephone can be seen as referring to a luxury life style (Barthes 1964, p.182). There are old-fashioned, bureaucratic, feminine and other kinds of telephones as well. Telephones may have features that in no way seem to relate to their practical function as a technical instrument.

The products have, in Barthes' view, a more restrictive meaning to begin with. A raincoat refers, first, to a protective function. In addition, it has meanings that exceed its practical function. It refers to other qualities as well (i.e., to climatic conditions and the weather). The product does not refer to such wider meanings simply by 'informing' the perceiver. The reference depends upon the perceiver and is always an interpretation bound to culture.

The functionalistic myth

Jean Baudrillard (1979, p.154 and 1981, p.167,172) has criticized the sign process and argued for a total change of a product's sign function. The sign has been pushed to the background or disappeared. The sign can therefore be compared with a map without reference. What is the use of such a map? If the referent of the sign disappears, what is the sign needed for anyway? (See also Aro 1985, p.61.)

The material product as a sign vehicle does not, in Baudrillard's opinion, represent and cover anything that could be interpreted. For example, pictures no longer need to be interpreted because they represent too much. They are too obvious and do not represent anything but themselves. Instead of representations they are simulations. A product (or a picture) simulates reality, but does not represent it. Disneyland, for example, does not represent something American and something having American qualities. Instead, it is a simulation. Disneyland is a Disneylandic place. It may be conceived as a 'new reality' a Disneyland reality.

Baudrillard (1987, p.9) has suggested that products should be examined according to their functions within a network of human actions in which the user is a control unit as, for example, in using the remote control of a television set. A car is transformed into a network of interactive control systems. It is controlled by an operator and it 'answers' to that operator.

But, is the reference to the product's use a sign at all? Barthes (1964) has attempted to answer the question by arguing that a tool refers to its use when the use is thematized. When the use is thematized, something other than its practical function is associated with it. For example, a net shopping bag used to carry things may refer to an Italian life style because such a bag is commonly used in Italy. The bag represents Italianness. It reminds people of an Italian way of living and may even indicate it. Accordingly, the use of the bag is thematized and it can be a sign referring to Italian life style, customs and people.

Similarly, children's toys can refer to cultural habits of doing and handling situations. Toys can express attitudes towards an activity. Children may adopt such references at an early stage if they are given toys that correspond to the things used by adults. Guided by cultural uses children's playing and toys are thematized (Barthes 1954–56, p.53). When a product is thematized, it is also semantized at the same time. A product begins to function as a sign, which refers to something other than its practical function. It may refer to a certain kind of activity, an attitude, or a cultural situation.

A telephone can connote a conversation (with the help of technology) and, at the same time, the transmission of speech to a remote place, possible contact with someone or something similar. As a tool the telephone is always perceivable in its materiality. And, on the other hand, a material object cannot function as a tool without representing something. The broad range of models on the market is a manifestation of various telephone representations. A telephone does not actually function as a simulation of speech communication, as merely a pattern of interactive control in Baudrillard's sense.

The intrinsic qualities (size, thickness of material, strength) of a product facilitate its identification. (Compare with Gibson's views presented earlier.) These qualities are determined by the use function (driving, hammering, sitting). The product possesses the qualities that make it a tool. Typical tools like hammers and scissors serve the forming of the material world. Their identity is determined from outside themselves.

A tool has a certain shape, solidity and the like, because the task that it performs requires it. Its shape is defined both by a proper fitness for the task and by alter-functionality (a term used in this context by Sonesson 1989, p.135–136). The requirements for its shape are alter-functional, but it possesses these qualities itself.

All objects that qualify for hammering are not conceived as hammers. It would be a situation in which only the intrinsic properties of the object would define its identity. Therefore, objects like chairs, for example, should be analysed according to their alter-functionality and not according to their intrinsic properties only. Therefore, the chair's other functions as a divider of a room, as an expression of the character of the room, as a reference of a life style should be taken into account as alter-functional qualities that affect its form.

The multi-layered sign

The sign is a reference relation that is interpreted in a certain situation. The semiotic sign in Peirce's philosophy is a generic concept and has several subclasses that can be characterized on the basis of their object relations (R–O) (Sebeok 1991, p.17). An index may include an iconic sign; a symbol may include both iconic and indexical signs. Especially symbols in design products may include more or less evident iconic signs, iconic signs that are more or less realistic in their representation. The degree of iconicity varies. For example, the colour of a product may refer as an iconic sign and the same colour may have a symbolic content. In addition, it can also be interpreted as an indexical sign (how the product was painted, how the colour has faded out). One mode of reference cannot transform into another mode; for example, an iconic sign cannot change into an index. Because of the different modes of reference in the object relation of the sign, the modes of interpretation vary as well in the R–I relation.

Indices are also relations that are interpreted as signs. It is sometimes conceived that all material artefacts are indices. I wish to look closer at this argument with the aid of a traffic sign. A traffic sign such as the general warning triangle is obviously a material artefact. It can be asked for what kind of sign, icon, index or symbol is it a material sign vehicle? Is it an index that is actually connected to its referent? If so, what kind of O does the warning triangle refer to as an index? As is already known, an artefact does not function as a sign only because of its physical existence. A person should look for its references and, in the case of an index, should look for an actual connection in its object relation. Otherwise the mere existence of this artefact could be interpreted in the following way. Its mere existence indicates 'something' worth noticing as the journey continues. Then all artefacts that draw attention on the side of the road could be indicators of something as a person proceeds. The warning sign would not differ from all the other material objects that are met. When travelling, people will obviously meet many real things, but they will not have specific indicators. In my opinion, then, the warning triangle does not function as an index at all. Instead it is a symbolic sign referring to a dangerous situation. Its warning form, a yellow triangle inside a red triangle, is a symbol (actually a symbol's replica) and it is interpreted on the basis of convention and agreement. The triangle has a symbolic meaning and is part of visual 'language' designed for traffic.

An iconic sign can be included in this symbol when, for example, a bump, a curve or an elk is drawn on the yellow surface of the triangle. An index that indicates a direction can be added to the symbol too (e.g., an arrow).

Symbolic meaning may sometimes be important and, at other times, weak. In other words, a symbol can convey significant meanings or be almost forgotten. It can be limited and known by a small group or it can be familiar to almost everybody.

A critique of the iconic sign

The iconic sign has been criticized for being a reference too loose for sensible interpretation (Eco 1979; Goodman 1976). All products can be considered similar to other products. Thus interpreting a product as an iconic sign would be trivial. The iconic sign would be empty because the product can be the sign of anything. For example, a white lighting fixture is similar to all other white things and similar to all other lighting fixtures as well. Critics have argued that iconic signs are not object relations based on likeness or similarity. The reference should instead be restricted in some way.

The critics therefore suggest that the representamen R and its object O have properties in common or they share the same properties. However, Eco (1979, p.192) has studied this argument exhaustively and has concluded that it does not hold. Eco claims that a picture of a thing and the thing represented in the picture do not have any properties in common. A picture depicting the nose of Queen Elizabeth does not share the properties of her nose. The two are different. At least, the iconic sign is not about the physical similarities between the picture and the real nose. Rather, an iconic sign provides an impression of similarity (Sonesson 1989, p.214).

In his thorough analysis of the (pictorial) iconic sign Sonesson (1989, p.250) concluded that the critics have applied a model from linguistics, and it has been misleading. Peirce has clarified his view about the relation between visual perception and language, which sheds light on this discussion as follows:

> . . . the object must be able to convey thought, that is, must be of the nature of thought or sign. Every thought is a sign.
> . . . "I saw it was red". Not at all. You saw nothing in the least like that. You saw an image, not resembling a proposition in the smallest particular. It instigated you to your judgement, owing to a possibility of thought; but it never told you so.
> (*CP* 1.538)

The critics have assumed that the iconic sign is symmetric even though it is often asymmetric. For example, when I see a car, I may recognize the similarity between its form (R) and a form of an insect (O), but it will not follow that I see an insect as a car (O).

The subjective quality of the iconic sign

Sign functioning is always interpretation. Therefore, for the sake of further development, the need for objectivity within a study must be examined. When an analysis fulfils the requirements for an objective method, it is possible to repeat the method and get the same results independent of the person carrying out the work. The results can be generalized and can be aimed at all corresponding events. Are the aims of this semiotic study the same: objectivity and generalizability? What is meant by these terms in this context?

The reliability of an analysis is one criterion for its objectivity. A reliable analysis does not permit too many random results. The objectivity of the analysis can be increased also by improving its validity (i.e., the question of how well the results correspond to the objectives of a study) (Niiniluoto 1980, p.139). Does the interpretation of a product as an iconic sign include too much randomness? If it does, the analysis would be unreliable, and it would not be objective. It would not even be valid enough because the reliability of an analysis also affects its validity (Eskola 1981, p.77). The lower the reliability, the lower the validity. An analysis with too many random variants is not a valid description of its object of study.

In applying the iconic sign of Peirce, I am interested in studying how an object may function as a sign when interpreted by a subject in a context (of use). The randomness of the results depends on the subjective quality of the interpretation. The thing interpreted, the design product, remains the same. I would, therefore, like to take a closer look at the subjectivity of the interpretation in the following discussion.

Subjective interpretation often means unreliability, for example, personal impressions (Anscombe 1976, p.8) or 'states of knowing' in the mind of an individual person (Niiniluoto 1980, p.138) that cannot be checked by external criteria. Then, a subjective interpretation includes something personal. How can a personal impression be considered reliable in an analysis and be accepted as part of it?

An impression is based on personal perceptions of a thing. The thing may be a percept common to many persons (as, e.g., a design product). But, it cannot be argued that these persons are talking about the same impression because they all have their own 'state of knowing' which the others cannot know anything about. The problem of the iconic sign seems to relate to this personal quality of interpretation. Personal impressions cannot be reliably repeated in an analysis, and another person is not capable of checking the analysis. Repetitiveness and control are basic requirements for an objective analysis in the natural sciences. But they are not ideals for semantic interpretation because then non-measurable percepts are being studied (Eskola 1981, p.52–53). The problem concerning repetitiveness and control might be of secondary importance in interpretations of iconic signs.

When someone perceives and interprets a product that is perceivable to others too, the object of perception does not afford itself only to one perceiver personally. A feature of the percept can be compared, but actually a 'state of knowing' is not being compared with someone else's 'state of knowing'. In fact, what is in question is the object and the impressions it furnishes. A perceiver of some products may say, for example, that 'these reds match'. Strictly speaking, the person should say: 'I see these reds match' (Anscombe 1976, p.16). Still the emphasis is on the object and not on the impression in the perceiver's mind.

An inner standard and external paradigm

But how is it possible that a common interpretation can be formed on the basis of people's different impressions when only one person can know what is being sensed? An answer to this question may be that one subject and a group of subjects have a similar inner standard or scale. The impressions are then applied to this scale. Another answer might be that a certain impression arises in a certain situation and context, and it can be experienced in a similar way by many subjects and can therefore be called a paradigm of the interpretation. A sense impression may have both an individual inner standard and an outer paradigm to determine its quality.

How can an inner standard guarantee that the interpreter is correct (gets the right impression)? The sense impression itself defines the standard. One impression is not sufficient. A second impression is needed for a comparison, and then a standard can be formed. How is the inner standard formed within a subject, and, second, how is it formed by the subject when the percept is directed to an outer object?

When I say I have a headache, how do I know that I am not mistaken? On another occasion when the headache is repeated, I can form an inner standard and classify my impression as belonging to the headache group and speak about it with other persons (Hintikka 1982, p.195–196). The classification requires recognition of the similarity between the two occasions and categorization. The recognition and categorization will continue on other occasions (of headaches) as well (Anscombe 1976, p.13). The inner standard is not rigid, however, and may change in scale.

The same phenomenon occurs in a situation when I remember something that happened to me during a performance. I will recognize the same sort of impressions during my performance, and I may compare the impressions and form an inner standard concerning my performances (e.g., amount of stress and pleasure).

An inner standard is also formed in a situation in which the percepts are dynamically interactive with the environment. The interpretation then focuses on something outside the subject (e.g., on a product). The interpretation likewise depends upon the habits, needs, motives, expectations and beliefs of the perceiver (Niiniluoto 1980, p.142). The interpretation is not, however, arbitrary or chaotic, but is usually organized in everyday experiences. This is due to the nature of the 'lifeworld', which Edmund Husserl has characterized.

> The lifeworld is the natural world – in the attitude of the natural pursuit of life are we living functioning subjects involved in the circle of other functioning subjects.
> (Husserliana IV, p.375, translated in Föllesdal 1990)

> The lifeworld even includes relations other than those to other persons. It is continually 'on hand' for me and I myself am a member of it. Moreover, this world is there for me not only as a world of mere things, but also with the same immediacy as a world of values, a world of goods, a practical world.
> (Husserliana III, p.59, translated in Föllesdal 1990)

The lifeworld is the natural world in which human beings live and to which everyday activities belong. It is the same for everyone, even though different people experience and understand it in different ways (Hintikka 1982, p.14–15; Föllesdal 1990, p.137–138).

A person's interpretation is formed in the lifeworld, partly by culture and partly by genetic factors. From a psychoanalytical viewpoint, culture also defines a person and his or her interpretation. In a semantic study it seems interesting to know that the unconscious is, according to Sigmund Freud, partly formed by culture, too. The preconscious filters meanings both to the unconscious and the conscious. Because the unconscious is formed as a counterpart to the preconscious, the former is likewise partly formed by culture. Therefore, part of the self is defined by culture and a product of culture. Jacques Lacan described the unconscious as an organized network of symbolic meanings. He referred to the various developmental stages of the subject. As children grow older and begin to use language, the subject becomes part of the symbolic order of the language, and, because it is included in this order, it cannot escape cultural values. A subject is, according to Lacan, totally included in a symbolic matrix of language. For example, family, dietary rituals, and conventions of dressing are symbolic orders. Language transmits these symbolic meanings as, for example, family anecdotes and names. The individual subject will be wholly included in these orders transmitted by language (Silverman 1983, p.73 and 164–167).

I have briefly touched upon this psychoanalytical viewpoint because even here cultural relations and influences are emphasized in interpretation (be it with a special emphasis on verbal language, and not on products, as is the case in my study). Other research, namely, a study of the meaning of things embodied in speech and writings, has been presented earlier by Csikszentmihalyi and Rochberg-Halton (1981).

I have discussed subjectivity and sense impressions as a part of semantic analysis because personal impressions play a role in the interpretation of iconic signs. An iconic sign is a sense impression, too. And it is unique and, at the same time, as in the case of colour interpretation, also depends on an outer paradigm. These two kinds of determinants, the personal inner standard and the outer paradigm, are affected by culture. In emphasizing cultural features in my analysis, I try to weaken the contradiction between the objective and the subjective in the semantic analysis of the sign.

A subjective interpretation of a product may form a standard and help comparisons of perceptions with each other and with other people's perceptions (Hintikka 1982, p 195–196). Thus the task of a semantic analysis is to afford possibilities for the comparison of perceptions, because the aim is not repetitiveness, controlled invariants or a measurable accuracy, as is the case in the natural sciences. The notion of the subjective quality of a semantic analysis is also a recognition of its limits. Subjectivity is characteristic for this kind of analysis, and it affects its results and the way in which they should be understood. The interpretation relation of the sign, the R–I, cannot be generalized too far so that it does not include subjectivity. A generalization would mean established and even fixed reference relations without a variation in subjective interpretations. And this cannot be the aim of a semantic analysis. Such an aim would not correspond to the Peircean sign either, which is a changing and infinite process (*CP*, 2.303). In analysing signs, a person does not seek for an idealized social subject. Instead the role of the context in which the sign functions is emphasized.

> Conscious really belongs to the subconscious man, to that part of the soul which is hardly distinct in different individuals, a sort of community-con- sciousness, or public spirit, not absolutely one and the same in different citizens, and yet not by any means independent in them.
> (Peirce 1896, p.47)

By a community consciousness Peirce means:

> . . . consciousness is not mere "immediate consciousness", . . . but is . . a sense of taking a habit, or disposition to respond to a given kind of stimu- lus in a given kind of way.
> (Peirce 1905, p.290–291)

Reliability of an iconic sign

The lifeworld has a general structure (Husserl 1970, p.139). Important and close things from the point of view of the interpreter are given priority over more dis- tant things. More familiar and common things in culture precede in their experience. Therefore, it is not surprising that everyday artefacts and natural objects in one's surrounding stand out in the interpretation of an iconic sign.

The same referents (O) of the iconic sign can appear in interpretations of different products because they are common and close to the perceiver. Such common iconic signs are, for example, references to facial features and expressions, to parts of the human body, to domestic animals and to other familiar natural objects such as trees and flowers, as well as to cultural artefacts such as comic strips and celebrities familiar from mass media. Such references in an iconic sign can appear frequently and convey meanings that, in addition to their familiarity, are close to people in the lifeworld.

Eleanor Rosch (1975) has studied such outstanding features of the lifeworld with the aid of what she called 'natural categories'. With psychological experiments she has shown that people are inclined to categorize objects around a prototype. The prototype represents typical characteristics of a certain group of objects and is the group's typical representative. The prototype has typical characteristics of its own. Such prototypes are formed in a culture, and they categorize objects similar to the prototype as belonging to the same group. Objects which differ from the prototype are classified into other groups, around other prototypes. Borderline cases are not clearly categorized at all because of the difficulty of determining the group to which the object belongs. Children show their abilities to categorize by depicting typical (prototypical) features of things in their drawings.

Recent psychological studies (e.g., Neisser 1987) confirm the results of Rosch's experiments and have not changed her conclusions about the natural categories around prototypes. New research has, in other words, complemented earlier results. The interpretation of an object as an iconic sign tells more about the interpretation than the result of a categorization does. The sign may refer to attitudes and beliefs related to the same object. Such conceptions and evaluations also define the qualities of the object. They are given priority or are dismissed in cat-

84

egorization. Typical features of an object are not, however, as stable in an interpretation as Rosch (1975) indicated. There are perhaps no stable representations at all. Categories vary and change.

There are other factors that can reduce the randomness of a semantic analysis. One of them is the competence of the perceiver. Experts in a particular field (geology, Egyptology, music, design) may, due to their background knowledge and experience, increase the reliability of their interpretations. An uncertain perceiver may ask for someone else's opinion and compare the interpretation to those of others (Anscombe 1976; see also Mäkelä 1990, p.54–55). Team work might be suitable for a semantic analysis in particular. But it does not completely eliminate the subjective part of an interpretation.

Cultural context

An interpretation with the help of the semiotic sign should always be considered in a cultural context in which meanings are transmitted (Eco 1979, p.73; Sebeok 1991, p.29). According to Eco (1979, p.26 and 46), semiotics is a general theory of culture in which the communication of signs requires, however, a study of their signification. A sign-vehicle can be interpreted as a semantic entity and placed in a semantic system. Thus signs are culture bound and their objects of reference are interpreted as 'cultural units'.

> A cultural unit is simply anything that is culturally defined and distinguished as an entity. It may be a person, place, thing, feeling, state of affairs, sense of foreboding, fantasy, hallucination, hope or idea.
> (Schneider (1968:2) in Eco 1979, p.67)

Signs are then interpreted in a certain way within a culture (a typical way, Rosch would say). There are cultures with typical features from which it can be identified. For the purpose of my analysis I shall conceive culture widely:

> Culture or Civilization, taken in its widest ethnographic sense, is that
> complex whole which includes knowledge, belief, art, morals, law, cus-
> tom, and many other capabilities and habits acquired by man as a member
> of society.
> (Tylor 1871, I)

When considered to be a culture-bound interpretation, the semiotic sign can refer to traditions of that culture (to its religions, political and economic conditions, industry and commerce, nature, etc.). A product can then refer as an iconic sign, an index and a symbol to cultural and natural things and events and it is meaningful to interpret a product in such a context only. One can, by following Eco's example (1979, p.27), interpret a car as a semantic entity when it is put into relation to other means of transport, such as other cars, bicycles or trains, and to other ways of travelling and moving, for example, a pedestrian and driver. The features that a car has in common with other cars, as well as those which distinguish it from other cars, define the car in a culture and as a part of a 'semantic field'. There can be several and contradictory semantic fields within a culture. Things may even have contrasting references to different objects (O) at the same time.

One problem of the analysis of a product is that references for any interpretation are too few or insufficient. The thing may be 'autistic' or 'inhibited'. Such reserved products have few signs. Consider, for example, a simple iconic reference like a gray box. It shows no indices, and it conveys no symbolic content of anything.

Another difficulty in the semiotics of design products might be the complexity and variety of their signs. The huge quantity of material artefacts offers so many different forms for interpretation, and the context of the interpretation may vary within the same culture. Modern pluralistic culture seems to hamper the interpretation of products analytically. Products are multilayered signs, and the different signs actually merge in one and the same product. How is it possible to analyse such multifaceted sign vehicles?

In a semantic analysis, knowledge of cultural features and values seems especially important according to research on different fields of knowledge. (See also Groupe μ 1995, p.38.) The question of randomness and unreliability can also be put in another way, when the interpreting subject is conceived as part of culture. People may then present culturally typical meanings in their interpretations. Then they do not emphasize the inner standard, the personal and individual aspect of a subject's interpretation. It may even be misleading to conceive a metaphorical interpretation as too personal and, then, as too random and unreliable for any analysis.

The reliability of an interpretation becomes actual and problematic when interpretations differ and are contrasted to one another. Which one of the interpretations is right or true? Which one is the correct metaphorical reference when several interpretations can be made? In a situation with divergent interpretations, a person would like to know who is right (which reference is correct). Behind such a question lies, in fact, another conception, namely, that one interpretation is more correct than the others, and the others are more or less erroneous. A situation like this does not permit but one correct interpretation of a product.

In a semantic analysis, however, the goal is not one correct interpretation. In the case of the metaphor only one correct unanimous interpretation (consensus) is not needed. A metaphor permits many interpretations by different people. Even a design product is 'polysemic' in this sense (Barthes 1964). The design product permits and affords many metaphors, which may vary in different persons' interpretations depending on knowledge, competence, cultural background, and personal history of reference. A product may cause several metaphors for one interpreter as well.

Is the variety of iconic signs within a culture broad after all? Products are interpreted according to 'natural categories' in the lifeworld. It can be concluded that common products have coherent intersubjective interpretations. An iconic sign is thus not fully arbitrary and does not necessarily vary much because inherent cultural features also define it. It is not defined on the basis of individual variety only

(Johansen 1993, p.289). Studies in sociology support this latter emphasis. Certain products correspond with groups of people who use these products. Coherent interpretations have a common socioeconomic base (Bourdieu 1986), due to the fact that products have social functions. (See also Paulsson and Paulsson 1956; Barthes 1964.) In using products a person exhibits himself or herself to other people. Equipment and decoration in a home and office, dressing and eating habits, transportation and routes, equipment for recreation, all tell something about a person in a concrete way through the products. People act with the help of products also socially, when they exhibit different sides of themselves to others. Other people perceive and interpret a person on the basis of the products used, and not only on the basis of what is said and the gestures made. A product can be seen as a statement, an assertion and an expression of a certain attitude, and it thus refers to a larger content than its practical function. The role of products as status symbols is well known. The references of products are, however, more complex. With the help of references traditional values that reside deep in a culture are strengthened, but one can also aim at changing values to meet new challenges in a new cultural situation.

Products have references due to the specific context in which they are interpreted. In commercial contexts they are seen as sales items, in museums as exemplary works, and in workshops as tools. The interpretation is affected by contextual expectations. It can be concluded that specific contexts will define the category in which the product should be interpreted and valued. Accordingly, an interpretation would be unqualified if the sign is not interpreted in an explicit context. From this reasoning it follows that the context must first be defined.

A semiotic process appears as a set of discoursive practices. Semiotic signs function in the discourses that speak of them as well as in those that analyse them. Because, in my study, sign functions have been analysed in the context of design (illustrated in chapter three), specific discoursive conditions have ben set that affect the relevance of possible interpretations (See Greimas and Courtés 1982, p.81;

Heiskala 1990, p.242). In the following presentation, I have worked out modes of sign references that are interesting from the perspective of design.

How does the interpretation proceed?

It is important to note that human perception is selective. When a person looks at a picture, some parts of it are depicted first.

> And what we call "reading" an image may perhaps be better described as testing it for its potentialities, trying out what fits.
> (Gombrich 1968, p.190–191)

> A few clues presented with sufficient boldness and clarity will make us find the solution of the puzzle which the image presents to us.
> (Gombrich 1968, p.197)

This quotation from Gombrich's analysis of the interpretation of pictures seems to support the conceptions of the lifeworld. An analysis of a picture begins with something which corresponds to a person's expectations (even though one has a first impression of the picture as a whole). Then the percept proceeds with a gaze to the other parts of the picture. Perception can begin from above, below, or from somewhere in between. There is no pregiven way for beginning an interpretation. A person's gaze shifts according to contiguity of the parts (Sonesson 1989, p.300). In this way, the parts of the picture, which may at first seem disconnected, are fused into a whole and a motif.

Although these psychological conclusions are about interpretations of pictures, they are, in my opinion, applicable to a three-dimensional product as well. Its interpretation can also begin from a detail and proceed to others as one gazes at it. The interpretation of a product does not start from a pregiven part. Instead a detail is fused into the interpretation of it as a whole and may refer as an iconic or indexical sign. Its details are, then, not disconnected, but thematized with the help of the references of the sign.

From the discussion in this chapter, I have drawn conclusions on how the semiotic sign is applicable to a design product in a semantic analysis. I have used the iconic sign to mean recognition of similarities between the representational form (R) and its object (O). It is a reference based on the recognition of similarity. A cultural context and natural categories of the lifeworld affect the interpretation of iconic signs and thematize them. The iconic sign is bound to culture and to the subjective impression as well. An iconic sign can be explicated and discussed with other people by relating the interpretation of the representational form to the material product. Other people may argue for another view without being incorrect. Their interpretations of the iconic sign are not necessarily erroneous even if they differ from mine. On the contrary, the specific and potential variety of iconic signs are important and interesting in the analysis. One should not try to eliminate this characteristic of a semantic analysis, but instead should pay attention to the arguments and ideas in various interpretations. Arguments concerning the iconic sign may exhibit attitudes and values inherent in culture and the lifeworld.

In the next chapter, I have worked out an application of a semiotic interpretation. A design product as a sign seems to offer possibilities for a multifaceted interpretation rather than leaving room for only one way of looking at it.

Different signs merge in a person's experience of a product. Signs do not function separately and individually, but form multilayered references. The complexity of the sign is increased because the references are not stable or fixed qualities of the product. I have conceived the representational qualities within the possibilities and limits of the iconic sign as well. The complexity and liveliness of the sign should be seen as a characteristic of the semantic analysis of a product. Since references of the sign can be interpreted differently at different times and in different situations, the analysis cannot be final and complete.

5 APPLICATIONS

I n previous chapters I have attempted to approach a semantic analysis of the design product. The definition of the four dimensions of the product seemed to be a good starting point. With this concept, I have aimed at an analysis in which different aspects of the design product can be taken into consideration while still being conceived as an integrated whole.

Now I would like to consider the sequence and order of the phases in applying the analysis. A semantic analysis of a design product requires knowledge of its other dimensions. An interpretation of the sign should be founded on such knowledge if it is to be a claim for validity. By connecting the interpretation of the sign to background knowledge and earlier experiences with the product type, I also aim at increasing the validity of my analysis; I try to add concrete aspects to the analysis as well, because the interpretation is about the design of concrete objects.

Background knowledge can contribute to semantic interpretation. For example, if a quality of the product seems to dominate, the background material may offer possibilities to take note of seemingly weaker references as well. I may then be able to take into account vague and contradictory references and the analysis will become more sensitive.

In semiotic analyses, a picture is divided into a plastic level and an iconic level (Sonesson 1989, p.150–179). The division resembles the starting point, namely, the division into syntactic and semantic dimensions. The syntactic dimension includes the product's technical structure and function, as well as its visual composition, which corresponds to the plastic layer of a picture (also called its syntax). Analysing the product's construction, visual components, details and relations, dynamics, rhythm, colour and other features of its syntax provides support for the interpretation of the product as a sign. Similarly, the plastic layer of a picture has been used as support for the interpretation of its iconic level.

The first step in my analysis was to collect background information about the product to be analysed. This procedure included going through the product's history. Information had to be gathered from various sources, such as museums, libraries, exhibitions, literature, brochures, stores, firms, institutions, and users. Information on products still in use continuously increases in quantity, and new models may have appeared on the market during the search.

Literature on and pictures of the product do not suffice for semantic analysis. In addition, I must be able to perceive and handle it as a three-dimensional arte-fact ready for use. I must be able to perceive it from many angles both during a period of time and at several different times. With these operations the perception process becomes complex as my impressions become enriched. The reliability of the analysis increases.

Because my object of study was familiar from the acquired background information already described, this kind of semantic analysis did not involve problems related to the recognition of a product never seen before. I did not attempt to reconstruct a situation in which the interpreter faces a strange product and tries to determine its purposes.

I have aimed at a systematic analysis to the extent to which I first considered the different parts of the material product, their technical and ergonomic functions, and well their visual composition. I analysed the product as it refers as a semiotic sign, an iconic sign, an index and a symbol. To carry out the analysis I opera-tionalized the functions of the sign. I made a list of different modes of reference with examples from semiotic (see, e.g., *CP* 2.274–2.302) and design studies and my own surroundings. In the semiotic literature, however, only a few examples were found from the design field.

I did not limit the quantity of possible modes of sign functions in composing the list. I tried, on the contrary, to present a broad variety of functions, as many modes as seemed relevant from a design point of view. The list included all in all twenty modes arranged in clusters of six iconic, nine indexical, and five symbolic functions. I have presented the list in a concise form for the sake of practicality. There is a risk, however, that the interpretation of a complex product will become shallow, thin and rigid. Many of the functions of the sign may whither away or break. Accordingly, there would no longer be enough references for a valid interpretation and the interpretation would be a stiff argument. To avoid such a situation, I formulated the functions in a nonformal way, and not in the form of a matrix or diagram. To enable the survey of the functions, I numbered the clusters.

The product as an iconic sign

1. The tradition of form

A product refers to its form tradition as an iconic sign. It may have a characteristic form of its own and specific features formed early in its history. Such a form will be recognized as an iconic sign, for example, a pair of scissors. The form of these scissors is not merely referring to the actual pair of scissors, but more generally to a form tradition of scissors or their prototype, to scissor-like forms, to scissorness. People do not interpret the quality of scissorness because they have seen the actual pair of scissors. They recognize scissor-like features in the actual product that they look at. In the same way, a product may represent a type of products as an iconic sign. The representational form connects it to a group of products, for example, cup-like containers.

2. Similar colour

An interpretation on the basis of colour may connect a product to ideas like an iconic sign. Colour may refer to a quality; for example, the colour white can refer to cleanness (a white stove is a clean stove). A light-coloured thing may refer to lightness so that the product looks lightweight.

All white things may refer to any white thing and to all the other white things, because they are similar in colour. Colour, then, seems to be too loose and broad a reference to function as an iconic sign. It does not seem to qualify for my list. It may be that only colour is not sufficient for a semantic interpretation of a product. The reference of a colour may rather be seen as support for the reference of the form. The role of colour in my interpretation will be to strengthen the functioning of a form as an iconic sign. Colour may function both together with the form and in addition to it. It may thus strengthen, for example, the reference to the form tradition of the product or to some other quality. If the role of colour is considered in relation to the form or even subordinate to it, its broad scope of reference will be reduced. Many references to other white products are then no longer relevant in the interpretation, and, for example, a white product does not function as a sign of all other white things.

Some close and important colours (coloured things) in the lifeworld may perhaps dominate the interpretation. They stand out. They stay in people's minds for a long time, so that people may even think the colours are permanent references. A product may then have a typical colour which characterizes it and which helps to categorize it. For example, the choice of an orange-red colour for a refrigerator does not look natural. In the same way, a brightly coloured thing may easily look like a toy.

The iconic sign of a colour can be mixed with its symbolic quality, which I deal with later.

3. Similar material

The material of a product can, according to the interpreted similarity, refer to some other thing as an iconic sign. For example, a gilded clock may refer to gold, whether it be real or not. Although it might be real gold, the material does not refer only to itself, but to other gilded things, to persons wearing them and occasions on which they are used. In this way something gilded achieves additional meaning in an interpretation and may indicate wealth, dignity and so on.

Like colour, the material of a product may be interpreted as an iconic sign. It then refers to a quality or state of affairs; for example, a glassy looking product may refer to fragility (other fragile things), a blistery surface to skin disease, and concrete to toughness and emotional coldness.

4. Metaphor

A product can be interpreted as referring through the resemblance of forms to another object in spite of different materials, construction and pragmatics. Such a metaphorical reference can connect two similar forms which differ in other respects. A metaphor functions like a substitute which appears, for example, as a person looks at an aeroplane in the sky and is suddenly reminded of something, maybe a bird or an insect. This experience can be described by words like 'look a bird-like plane', 'a nose-like a bill', 'sharp-pointed like a stinger'.

A familiar example of a metaphor in design literature is the car referring to an insect, for example, the Volkswagen when it is seen as a beetle. The perceived form of the car (R) refers to the form of a beetle (O). A car may function as a metaphor when it shows a smiling face, as was the case in car design especially in the 1950s. Klöcker (1980, p. 204) (figure 24) has illustrated product metaphors and conceives the associations as negative for design purposes.

Figure 24. Examples of metaphorical references by Klöcker (1980, p.207–208).

Common utensils such as the vacuum cleaner may have features designed to be similar to those of space ships and racing cars. They are conceived as master products because they are technically more developed and look grand and impressive. Common things are therefore designed to resemble master products with similar features. The design of the vacuum cleaner may give the impression of having the same qualities as the master product. A vacuum cleaner may thus seem technically highly efficient and fast moving. Products designed for children may have features borrowed from master products as well. These might be figures from comic strips, pedagogical tools, equipment in adventures and weapons. This kind of reference design is close to styling.

Even the size of a product can be conceived as an iconic sign, as a metaphor. For example, a small chair can be associated with a child's chair and have qualities belonging to a child's environment and use. This impression may be supported by colours.

5. Style

The product form may refer to a group of forms, a style. A style is more or less defined as a whole. Its parts relate to each other through the resemblance of form within the pregiven style. By 'style' I mean the so-called style periods familiar from art history, for example, l'art nouveau and Biedermeier, as well as trends of fashion, for example, safari-look and Marlboro Classics. In addition, stylistic features may refer to a certain period in time, a sub-culture, a local tradition, a social event and a life style, for example, the hippies and the hip-hop.

Forms and proportions are features that refer to the same object O, which is the style. Products with different functions are included in a style and they are associated as iconic signs on the basis of formal features. Thus a style is a whole that determines its parts, but it may include many kinds of forms. A style can be recognized on the basis of forms supported by their colours. In design, stylistic descriptions are used frequently to characterize a product and its appearance. A geometric categorization of the product form into spherical and square products may also be a stylistic description of it, even though a mere sphere style is not a common label.

6. Similar environment

A product can be interpreted as referring to a specific environment on the basis of similarity. It refers in a coherent way with references of its surroundings. According to these references the product is conceived as adapting itself and belonging to an environment. A component of a specific environment, for example, a kitchen, may influence other components designed for it. One may talk of kitchen products designed in accordance with the kitchen milieu (Schürer 1969, p.20).

The product as an index

1. The trace of a tool

A detail of the form can refer to a tool by means of a trace used in the manufacturing process and a method of production. In the same way a colour can function as an index. A person sees the trace of colouring and concludes the method and tool of colouring.

2. A pointing form

The form, detail, or position of a product can point in a direction which indicates its technical function or use function. It can be interpreted as pointing at something. The dynamics of the form directs a person's gaze in a certain way. An index might point at a detail for grasping the product and at a position of the detail required for the grasping. A product may have indexical signs for pushing, pressing, lifting, turning and the like. A designer may add an index to indicate such functioning, for example, an arrow or another graphic figure or texture. The position of a press button or a pedal may indicate the direction of its function.

3. Marks of use

A product may have traces of abrasion in its form and colour. Traces of use appear as dents and flaws, repairs, trash, dirt and so on. Newness appears in opposition to the traces of use.

4. Other traces

Other traces, like rust spots, corrosion, drops of water, or stains can be perceived on the product's form, and may indicate its material quality and external circumstances.

5. Light and sound signals

Light and sound signals attract attention as indices, and usually they refer to a technical function. For example, a red light on a stove may indicate when the oven has reached a certain degree. The light goes out when the oven has the indicated temperature.

6. Sound of use and noise of a product

The buzz from the motor of a car may be an index of its departure. The noise from moving a chair may indicate a person leaving the room. The product may even have designed details to prevent the noise of use, as, for example, rubber pads. They have no structural or functional meaning for its performance as an instrument, only meaning for diminishing noise.

7. Smell of a product

Usually the smell of a product refers to its material and actual functioning. From the smell of a cleanser a person can deduce that the room has been cleaned recently.

8. Touch of the material

The quality and condition of the material of a product may refer as an index through the sense of touch. For example, the temperature of a radiator (the radiation) indicates that its valve is open. By lifting a product, a person can decide whether it is empty or not.

9. Graphic figures on the product form

Figures drawn on the form may refer the real functions of the product and be in actual connection with corresponding details. Peirce's examples are the yard stick (*CP*, 2.286) and notices to Marines (*CP*, 2.288), both of which are actually connected to their indicated objects O.

Symbols of a product

1. Graphic symbols

The name and logotype of the company are symbols which refer to the manufacturer (e.g., the combination of letters K R U P S). In the same way, letters and numbers are symbols of a certain model and range of products; they distinguish them from other models. Markings on the form may also be symbolic signs as, for example, a word and a graphic figure (on-off, Rec., *, + and -).

2. Symbolic colour

A product's symbolic colour may refer to a cultural habit; for instance, black objects in Finnish funeral ceremonies refer to sorrow. The red carpet belongs to another kind of ceremony. The content of the symbolic reference must be known to enable its understanding and use. The symbolic colour is learned. In this sense, it differs from a colour as an iconic sign, which may be a personal impression of a possible meaning.

3. Symbolic forms

The symbolic sign is not interpreted according to referential similarity or an actual connection between the perceived form and its object, but, instead, according to cultural habit. Any form can in principle be a symbol of anything. In cultural practice, however, symbols do not function that freely. Symbols are first established by people, then they are made known, and, after that, they might function and be useful. A ticket is a piece of paper that functions as a common symbol (actually the paper is a replica of the symbol). The meaning of the ticket conveys a message agreed upon. The symbolic sign means 'this piece of paper (replica) shows you that I have paid to get in'.

4. Symbolic positions and postures

A product may have a symbolic position and posture. Its position may have a conventional meaning, as when a person places the fork and knife on the plate to mark the fact that he or she has finished eating. The position of handles and signals may indicate that a door is locked. A signal may indicate an invitation. Rules of games are symbols. In games and sports the posture of a piece of equipment may have symbolic meaning. The high stick position, slashing, in ice hockey has as its consequence a punishment of two minutes on the bench, even though no actual harm was done.

A product may convey iconic symbols; in other words the symbol includes a visual similarity to its content such as a feather as a symbol of light weight. Many souvenirs function as iconic symbols, like the Eiffel Tower referring to Paris. The miniature object looks like the Eiffel Tower, but it does not refer to the building in Paris only, but to the whole city and to memories of a trip to Paris. It may even represent France and the French.

5. Symbolic material

The material of a product may function as a symbolic sign, as, for example, the wine in Communion refers to blood and further to mercy. Rice in a wedding refers to fertility and to happiness for the married couple. Materials of dresses may refer to a social status and to the character of an event (e.g., the mink wall at a premiere).

The iconic, indexical and symbolic modes of the references of a sign have been summarized in appendix 1.

Choice of examples for the application

The examples for the analysis have been selected to illustrate how this approach can be applied to characterize design objects. The main point is not to define a product as functioning as a specific sign. With the product examples I try to present different modes of sign functioning and compare them. Therefore, I have chosen examples according to differences in use, size, and environment. They should be common and familiar industrially manufactured products on the market with a wide range of users. I have tried to avoid focusing on special cases that would affect the validity of the analysis and hamper application to products other than those chosen for study.

Because the products chosen as examples for my analysis do not have a limited and specified target group of users, the users do not determine them as special cases.

The examples should also be typical design products. Such objects have been designed by more than one designer in many countries. They have appeared in design magazines. They have been exercises in the education of designers.

In addition to the design viewpoints, I have considered possible public interest in my choice of the product example. External conditions and the products environment have also affected the choice. Their milieus of use should vary in order to enrich the analysis. The degree of freedom of form should be considered. I have avoided products that are classified as especially technical or artistic because I did not want to emphasize these qualities from the start. Later on, it may be interesting to widen the application to technical and artistic products in particular. At this early stage, these qualities have been deliberately ignored. Then it may be possible to see whether they appear anyway and how their appearance occurred. The fact that I have not emphasized artistic qualities in the choice of examples does not mean that design products do not have any. They may reside behind more apparent features because the practical function seems more important. I have applied my analysis to products other than those that have been studied earlier. (See the list in appendix 2.) Rather, I have contributed to the material and consider other products for my application. I have used other products because the conclusions drawn earlier may lead my analysis, in correspondence with them, in the same direction. Furthermore, I have not wanted to connect my analysis to the same examples because my work would easily become a mere critical examination of earlier results. I have, however, made use of earlier approaches in this study. I have chosen the following four products as examples:

— the steam iron, which is a common electric hand tool
— an exercise cycle, which is measured for the whole body and is used in at least two distinct environments
— a telephone kiosk, which is a public design outdoors into which a person can enter
— a bicycle helmet, which is a thing to be worn outdoors.

Practical consideration like size and availability did not influence my choice because I found suitable examples without a problem. Consumer tests or marketing research did not affect the choice either, although they provided useful background material. Evidently, there are other household items suitable for this analysis, like the toaster and the electric mixer. I chose the iron because it was a commoner utensil and appeared more frequently in design contexts. Consumer analyses had been made of some other household items as well, for example, the microwave oven (Kanerva 1988). I still preferred the iron because its freedom of form seemed more suitable for a start than the basic square form of the oven.

Radios, calculators, mobile telephones and the like could be interesting objects for a semantic analysis too. Rapid technological changes have radically influenced their design, as has already been pointed out by Lannoch and Lannoch (1983) and Gros (1984a). Miniaturization of electronic components is, however, only one parameter that influences design. Aspects concerning freedom of form affected my decision to choose products other than these for my analysis. Mobile telephones, which are successful Finnish design products, have been studied elsewhere (Pulkkinen 1994). I also considered four examples enough because I did not want to burden the study with too much sample material. Too many examples could easily blur the main objectives of the study and emphasize the role of the particular products, which were chosen as examples to illustrate sign functioning.

There were many different models of the chosen examples on the market. For the analysis of the steam iron, I chose a group of 12 examples. A comparison of different models was then possible within the study. The other product examples were examined with the focus on one representative. But they were analysed in comparison with other models on the market.

The steam iron

A steam iron is a typical design product with regard to the given requirements. It is frequently used as an example in design literature and textbooks (Selle 1978, p.187; Larroche and Tucny 1980, p.168 and p.178; Radice 1984, p.22; Manzini 1986, p.121; Sparke 1987c, p.53; Aldersey-Williams 1988, p.21, 50 and 94; Atkinson & Mockford 1991, p.42; Bürdek 1991, p.221; Garner 1991, p.28 and 52;

Quarante 1994, p.514). A steam iron has even been given the status of an example when the importance of design has been illustrated in a textbook (Burden et al. 1988, p.44–47). The creative process of design has been illuminated with the design of a steam iron as an example (Archer 1954, p.15; de Noblet 1993, p.26). And finally the steam iron has been a popular exercise in design schools (Reese 1985, p.23; Lindinger 1990, p.95). For my analysis I tried to find the same examples that had earlier been analysed in a user test (Aalto 1986), since the test results would have been directly applicable to my analysis as background material. This was not, however, fully possible, because the models of steam irons had changed and the same models were no longer available in 1989. (See appendix 3 for a comparison of the models of the test in 1986, the models of my analysis in 1989, and more new models in 1994.)

The examples of steam irons used in this analysis are 1) AEG DB 402, 2) AEG DB 309, 3) Braun PV 63, 4) Braun PV 64, 5) Moulinex 3600, 6) Rowenta DA 21, 7) Rowenta DA 23, 8) Rowenta 32, 9) Rowenta DA 32, 10) Philips HD 1464, 11) Philips HD 1462, 12) Tefal Compact 15L model 14.31. See appendix 3 for the technical and ergonomic aspects of the steam irons.

The iron was one of the first electric household appliances. In the end of the 19th century the first models appeared on the market (Canby 1963, p.80; Strandh 1979, p.224; Hardyment 1988, p.73). Earlier there had been hollow irons heated with coal or with a piece of iron. These early irons had a handle

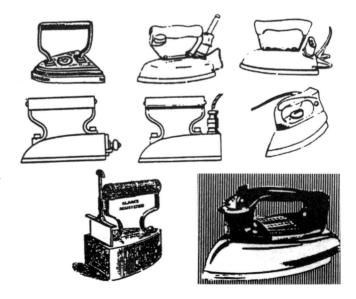

Figure 25. Old models of irons.

and a lock with hinges. They easily made the washing dirty and they were not very handy in other respects either. After this type of iron, the so called flat irons with two changeable bases to a handle appeared on the market (Lyytikkä et al. 1963, p.14). The early electric iron models resembled these pre-electric objects (Sparke 1987b, p.87). (See old iron models in figure 25.)

In the 17th century the iron often had a round front tip. Later, the tip was designed to be

Figure 26. A model of a divergent iron from France in 1954 (Larroche et Tucny 1980, p.38).

sharper. The form of the sole plate has been triangular since the 18th century. In Finland, irons were designed similarly, that is with a sole plate sharp in the front and broad at the back. In the United States, however, irons were made with a sharp point at the back as well. They were convenient for ironing sleeves and fronts of shirts because the iron did not have to be turned during the operation. In France an iron was designed with a sole plate that continued upwards as a heel; it is shown in figure 26.

Thermostats were added to irons in the 1920s. The steam irons that appeared on the market in the 1950s are also irons with thermostats. They resembled common flat irons, but had a water tank and steam vents in the sole plate to allow the cloth to be steamed during ironing. The benefit of steam irons is the all-around use for both steam ironing and dry ironing.

Technically the new electric steam irons differ from the old irons. From the 1960s on the supply voltage has been 1000 W. The sole plate is usually made of a light metal alloy and chrome-plated steel. Because irons were heavy tools earlier, it is often believed that they should be heavy tools to function better. The conception has, however, proved to be wrong because the requirements for better results in ironing are a high temperature and humidity (Palsanen 1958, p.142; Lyytikkä et al. 1963, p.12; Hardyment 1988, p.74).

A steam iron has a water tank on the sole-plate or in the front. Its handle connects the pointed front to a broader heel. The heel is usually triangular and smooth in order to function as a base between the operations and during storage. The controls are somewhat standard and the markings are fairly well standardized, too. However, this feature does not mean stagnation in their design; new models are being produced at a good pace. A saturated market requires some kind of model differentiation and new technical details for a product to be competitive. But the market does not fully explain such a vast variety of irons. The companies also have their own tradition that they follow in their development of irons. They also have different design strategies that are not necessarily regulated to fill momentary gaps in the market. Trends in iron design can be studied by analysing chronological shifts as part of a company's strategy.

In a situation of saturated markets design becomes the main competitive tool for the company. It seems profitable to produce only irons that sell well for certain. In addition the producer sells to the retailer rather than directly to a user (Samson 1988).

There have been only a few technical innovations, but many different models of irons. According to a brochure the Rowenta iron is the market's pet. The Tefal 15L is, according to its brochure and package text, best in tests. The Braun, according to its advertisement, is a smash hit.

The development of other household items may have influenced the form of the steam iron. Companies present their "white goods" together, and they must all fit within the line. In addition, manufacturing techniques and materials have changed the appearance of irons. A new environment of use may also bring new qualities to the form of an iron, for example, the travel (steam)iron, which then may influence the usual domestic iron. The travel iron has a joint in the handle for bending, and it is smaller and more colourful than the normal iron. Due to their bright colours they are easily linked with products for sport and leisure and less easily to domestic items (figure 27).

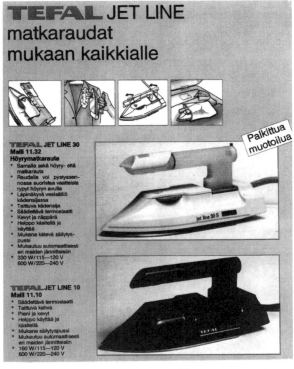

Figure 27. Travel (steam)irons.

Consumer research on irons and steam irons

Ironing is one of the most time-consuming activities in washing clothes. Research into the use and marketing of irons has emphasized initiatives to ease and speed up the work (figures 28 and 29) (Giedion 1948, p.571; Lyytikkä et al. 1963, p.9; Aalto 1986, Kristofferson Sandström 1993, Ehrnrooth 1994).

Speed and ease are emphasized in the pictures of packages (figure 30) and in brochures and marketing.

In a comparative study of irons in Finland in 1962 (Lyytikkä et al. 1963), 17 irons were analysed, four of which were steam irons (figure 31).

Twenty years later the Research Centre for Household and Consumer Matters in Finland studied all 22 steam iron and 13 dry iron models on the market (Laine 1983). Since then, there have been many rapid changes in the form of irons. The number of steam irons increased, and steam control was added. Therefore, a new study was carried out in 1986 by the same centre (Aalto 1986); 12 new models were analysed. At the same time there were about 30 steam iron models on the market. The material was chosen from the most complex models of a company's range. Technical qualities were measured, and ease of use was evaluated by

Figure 28. An advertisement of an iron in 1850 (Giedion 1948, p.572).

Figure 29. The marketing of an iron in 1909 (Giedion 1948, p.572).

Figure 30. Tefal and Braun packages in 1989.

14. Hoover   15. Morphy-Richards   16. Rowenta   17. Vakes

Figure 31. Four steam irons analysed in 1962.

109

a jury. The jury considered the quality of use to be good and easy on average. Three of the irons were considered excellent (5 points). In the tests no major differences appeared between the models. Meisner and Röhl (1994), however, have found a major difference in the durability of irons.

The information unit of Helsinki Energy has published guidelines for consumers. The importance of the form and handle of an iron are noted. In addition, the consumer should pay attention to the balance, controls, supply voltage, weight, length of cord, storage, price and import agency. Ironing, durability and maintenance were not dealt with. The publication (1994) lists, all in all, 41 different steam iron models. (Compare with 32 models in 1988 and 29 models in 1993 of the lists by Helsinki Energy.)

Even today, the iron is considered to be dangerous. Figure 32 is the cover of the British magazine Design (1989, p.30) dealing especially with product safety. A typical example is the iron. A heated iron has burned users' hands, damaged cloth, and even lit a fire. Thus the design and marketing of new irons aims at presenting a safe product. A pilot light, sound signal, and other safety features have been added to the iron.

Figure 32. The cover of the Design magazine (No.482, 1989).

Steam irons as signs

In the following discussion I analyse the examples of steam irons as signs and I present my interpretation according to the application of iconic signs, indices and symbols.

A distinct metal or black sole plate refers, as an iconic sign, to the form of old irons and the form tradition of irons as, for example, in figure 33. From such a reference it can be concluded that the iron represents 'many years of experience'. Also in marketing, emphasis is placed on experience, as, for instance, in the text on the AEG package: according to good experience ('aus Erfahrung gut').

Both the sole plate and the handle refer to the form tradition of an iron because they are designed as distinct components. With this partition of the form, the product refers to a thing to be taken seriously, as the common tool traditionally is, in a matter-of-fact way. The product expresses the attitude that the practical function is of primary importance. There are, however, also other kinds of models among the chosen examples. They do not clearly refer to form tradition. Instead, the aim has been to leave tradition behind and introduce a new form. Instead of a traditional form the product is presented under the company's trademark.

Figure 33. An iconic sign of an iron referring to form tradition.

The brand product refers to the company as, for example, the Braun iron refers to high quality through the reputation of the Braun firm. The product has a 'Braun form'. The iron is a Braun-like product. A divergent form like that of the Rowenta is more traditional and, at the same time, is easily recognizable as a brand product as well.

The white colour of irons refers to the environment of use in the kitchen and to the other white products in the kitchen. Good households are shown with white interiors in advertising and design magazines. The interiors are equipped with white utensils. They seem clean and tidy, which is advantageous if, at the same time, one wants to emphasize a hygienic environment, which easily shows trash and dirt. (See, e.g., the Philips brochure with an inviting kitchen, 1988).

Shelves in department stores present the same trend. Household appliances are white goods. The companies have a white product line, which differs from their black line for consumer electronics. With the help of colour a person relates the products to each other and to other products in a similar line. Products that deviate from the line stand out. They may differ from other models with other references. For example, hygiene may not be the foremost quality. Thus these products may be associated with other qualities, which are not preferred in the context of washing and ironing, or they may seem unsuitable and confusing in a more general sense.

The white colour of a coherent iron form, in which the handle form continues unbroken down to the sole plate, exemplifies an iron of the 1980s, at least in Finland. Desirable features such as light weight, ease of use, speed, smoothness and the like have been the main ideas of their design. As a result, the iron has a harmonious white and smooth form. Rowenta deviates, however, from this design concept. Still, it has been very successful on the market. A characteristic feature of the Rowenta iron is the water tank in a smoky gray colour. Its form can be associated with the dominant white line on the basis of the white handle, which is another characteristic part of it.

Steam irons are not quite white in colour, but have shades of gray. They do not, strictly speaking, have the same colour at all. But this fact does not seem to influence the overall impression of whiteness.

Two of the examples are grayish blue in colour (though of differing shades). This feature does not make them seem cheaper than the white models, however.

On the contrary, they look more expensive and more exclusive on the basis of the colour shade in comparison with the commoner irons. But, when an iron has many different coloured control buttons and graphics like the AEG 402 and has a colour-ful expression, it may refer to cheap mass products expressing low quality.

The colour of details seems relevant, for example, the water blue, black or gray spray buttons, which could easily be related to the colour of water. The colour of the water tank and other colour markings relate to water as well. The buttons for more steam are usually red and orange, which may refer to heat and additional heat, which also seems relevant, because the shot of steam requires a hotter iron.

Surprisingly, then, the Tefal model has a contrasting design. The spray button is pink and the steam button was pale blue. This difference was perhaps motivat-ed by the connection of the steam button to the control plate of the same colour. The pastel shades of the Tefal buttons can also be considered to refer to a user group with potentially feminine preferences or to an imagined use environment with pastel shades of colour.

Many different kinds of expressivity and 'physionogmic references' can be seen in irons. For example, the contrasting colours of black and white in the front of the AEG 402 makes the form look like a pessimistic, sour face because the con-trast of colours is a line downwards as in a negative mimic expression. The front of the irons can be interpreted as a bill or an open mouth. The black water tank opening of the Braun iron can be considered an open mouth, and the expression of the whole iron looks like something shouting. The front opening of the Moulinex tank looks like a mouth with lips. When looking at the irons from the front a person can associate them with features of similar animal forms. The black buttons of the Braun at the top of the form seem like ears.

All of the irons look like forward moving things on the table. Some of them seem to point actively forward. The more plastic the form, the more moving its looks, as, for example, the Braun and the AEG 402. In an upright position the irons look different. They have a surrendering or pleading expression. The handle of an iron may look like a pouch or sac filled with something. In a package the iron is shown as flying in the air.

Style

It is easy to recognize the iron style of the 1980s from the models. They have characteristics in common, like a smooth light coherent form with distinct colourful control buttons. The Philips iron can be especially characterized as having a practical style because the different parts seem plainly corresponding to the functions. The details of its form, the handle, the water tank, the spray button, seem neutral and without any special expressivity. There is no special shade of colour or text. One might call the design engineering style defined by production and technical details such as joints and seams of moulds.

The form can look as if it has been sculptured from clay. It acquires then a style that could be named sculptural because it has smooth transmutations between its parts, rounded forms combined with sharp cuttings.

The Braun iron seems to refer to forms familiar from ships and as having a ship style, for example, the roundness of the water tank opening, the oval form of the front that reminds one of a ship's smokestack. This ship-like form is supported by the white colour and the dynamic form (figure 34).

Indices of steam irons

Traces of production such as seams of moulds can be seen in plastic and metal parts of the iron, as can other marks made on it by the tools of its manufacture.

The iron often has a special design for the grip and the thumb. The grip and the direction in which the controls are operated is indicated by indices. Indices are

114

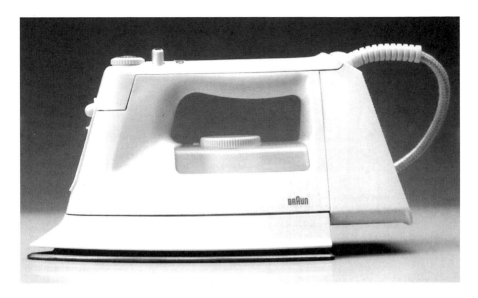

Figure 34. A ship-like iron.

designed for lifting, turning, pulling, especially on buttons, temperature selectors, and steam control dials. The selector is grooved to give the user a better grip and better adjustment and, it can be associated with an object that can be turned as a wheel. This reference is emphasized by an arrow or line marked beside the selector. The buttons of the AEG 309 and Tefal are slanting and grooved to indicate their push function. The removable water tank of the Rowenta has a special design for the grip, namely, a circular form or a grooved texture on both sides. The spray nozzle of the water tank opening in the front part of the iron indicates the direction of the spray. The overall form of the iron indicates a direction forwards. A form pointing in a direction as an indexical sign can also be misleading. For example, the scant cutting of a button may direct the movement of the hand forward, but it will also show that it can only be pushed down. The cause for the scant design has not been to guide the finger, but to give more space for the finger to move forward and reach the steam button in front of it. Therefore, the scant form becomes merely a transmutation from one form to another.

The water line on the transparent tank indicates the amount of water in it. Six of the twelve chosen examples had a pilot light to indicate their warming up.

One iron has a warning sound to indicate when it had been left in a horisontal position for too long (30 seconds) or in an upright position for 10 minutes. It is called a 'rational iron'. Indices of the iron are also sounds of use, as, for instance, the soft tinging when the temperature selector is turned. When the spray button is pushed, a small rushing sound can be heard, and the user can decide whether or not the water tank is filled or empty.

The heat of the sole plate can only be tested by estimating the time for its cooling or by touching it.

The form of the handle can refer as an iconic sign to the grip; there is a similarity between the handle and the grip. The form of the handle also seems to continue into the grip. The handle affords gripping, and thus both the similarity of the forms (handle form and grip form) and the continuation of the handle form are seen at the same time. The reference is a combination of iconic and indexical signs. The similarity of the forms supports the direction of the continuation. In the same way the sole plate of the iron affords ironing when the smooth plate is perceived in relation with a smooth table surface (the cloth in between). There is both similarity of forms and continuation.

Symbols of the steam irons

I found surprisingly many symbols in the steam iron models. The manuals included the same symbols and also explanations of their meaning. The symbols are easy to name. They are figures, words and markings on the form. The name and logotype of the company are well displayed on all of the models. In addition, the Rowenta has 'Made in Germany' on its form. The functions of the controls are shown by symbols such as a cloud for steam, two clouds for a shot of steam, rays for water spray, a steaming iron for cleaning the iron, and various lines and dots for adjustment. Many words, letters and numbers, such as perfect, secure, protector, comfort, auto, electronic, 3600, 200, 400, and S seem to refer to high technology and power (automatic, auto, jet, 3600). They may have other connotations, like upper class (jet set), high tech products (a jet plane) and a new era, as well. They may also refer to flexibility, freedom of choice, additional value (variojet, plus) and so forth.

The symbols seem to enrich the form. This enrichment can easily be seen when the iron is turned so that the user can look at the other side. The iron is designed with the front side as a facade with symbols and with the other side empty. The composition of the symbols resemble ornaments, and thus they have a decorative function as well.

On the other hand, the Braun iron is an example of a scarce use of symbols. The brand name Braun is emphasized. Its other symbols are reduced to a few plain colour dots on the controls.

The symbols add information and practicality to the appearance of the irons. And they emphasize the style and the technical character of the irons. The irons are easy to distinguish from one another on the basis of their different symbols.

Some of the symbols can be classified as iconic symbols when the conventional meaning is supported by a figure that resembles it. Many controls had such an iconic reference.

The sign function of the iron becomes more apparent when the different models are compared. One product seems different when examined beside another. The iconic signs may be strengthened or may change. For example, the Philips represents the 'small and handy' type of iron. It shows little expressivity. Seen in the group of irons, this characteristic is emphasized, and the Philips seems even more neutral and commonplace than when it is examined separately. The characteristic features of the AEG 309, the Braun and the Rowenta are emphasized in the group of irons in a manner similar to that of the Philips. The most typical features of a model seem to become more emphasized in a group.

When irons are grouped into pairs, the distinct features of a model appear more clearly. This differentiation is important from a semantic point of view because these features dominate in an interpretation. It is easy to couple the models on the basis of a chosen characteristic. For example, the Braun and Tefal easily made a pair of white smooth coherent irons in the group. Rowenta and Philips made another kind of pair, of angular forms. The AEG 402 and the Braun can be coupled on the basis of their smooth form in front. The Braun and Rowenta were pairs because of their distinct metal bottoms. Pairs with opposite features are also useful, such as those of the Braun and Rowenta and the AEG 309 and the Moulinex, because deviating features are easy to note.

The examples used were common steam irons on the market in Helsinki in 1989. They can be compared with earlier and newer models in 1994 (appendix 3), and the changes in iron design can be determined. It seems that changes are not made in just one direction. There is more than one trend and they may even oppose each other. A trend towards a more coherent overall form is apparent (see also Klöcker 1980, p.139), along with another trend of regression. The regressive feature comes from an earlier model, or rather from its form history, and has been applied to a new model. For example, some new irons have a heavy looking black border of plastic at the bottom. It refers to the form tradition of irons as heavy tools (also firm, solid, durable). Furthermore the form may connote familiar, secure and reliable things. The new Braun model, the PV 53 (1990), has a dark gray bottom design in this manner (figure 35). The model deviates from the white overall forms of the earlier Braun irons and opposes aims of Braun design, such as simplicity, smoothness and lightness.

An iconic sign may last even in a comparison within a group. However, by looking at the examples several times over a period of time may reveal new signs. For example, the Braun iron seemed to correspond to a ship style. This impression did not change in my interpretation. The reference seemed to fade, however, when I got used to the idea, and after a while I did not pay much attention to it. However, I may start perceiving another kind of sign function, for example, a mimic expression (of a being). This is not a symbolic reference. The sign is interpreted as a metaphor. When the

Figure 35. Braun Special PV 53, 1990.

irons are examined from the front, they seem to approach the perceiver. This dynamics is apparent in pictures as well (figure 36).

The details of an iron can also function as signs and momentarily shift their references. For example, the spray button of the Philips seems for a while like a Lego brick.

A smooth sole plate is one of the most important parts of an iron from the point of view of its use. Its quality is emphasized in marketing. At first, the sole plate seems to show only little expressivity, because it is usually looked at from the side, especially the right side. In an upright position the sole plate is revealed. Its most

Figure 36. Iconic signs of steam irons from the front.

easily damaged part appears. It is surprising to note that it lacks all kinds of protection, like a cover. A damaged or dirty sole plate and the blockage of its holes directly influence the quality of use and the result of use (the quality of ironing).

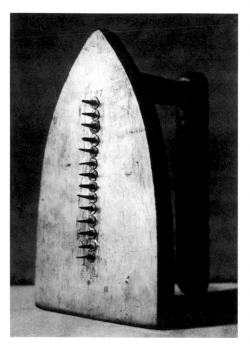

Figure 37. 'Le cadeau', object and photograph by Man Ray, 1921.

The iron has been used as an objet d'art (Man Ray 1980) (figure 37). The context of art has changed its pragmatic dimension, and, therefore, also the semantic dimension has changed. The iron as an art object differs from the iron as a design product. The artist has recognized the most sensitive and vulnerable part of the iron as an iconic sign. He has fastened a few sharp thorns for 'defense'. At the same time the iron was changed into a non-iron that cannot be used for ironing.

The exercise cycle

The second example is an exercise cycle, which differs in many ways from the first example, for instance, with respect to use, technical function, size and measurement. Both examples have the home environment in common. The exercise cycle is, moreover, especially a piece of equipment suited for fitness and conditioning schools.

The exercise cycle has been recognized for its design in professional design magazines (Industrial Design 1984, Salovaara 1988). It has been a popular task in the education of designers, for instance, in Ohio State University, 1986 (form 115, 1986), and at Hochschule für Gestaltung in Halle, 1988 (Hufnagl 1991, p.43).

The first exercise cycle in Finland was meant for the rehabilitative treatment of patients. It was called the stationary cycle. Professor Dodo Rancken, who worked in a surgical clinic in Helsinki, bought the cycle in Germany in the beginning of 1900 and lent it to his patients for a small fee. The cycle was used in hospital until the 1960s and was then included in the collection of the Museum of Medical History in Helsinki.

The first manufacturers of exercise cycles were companies of usual bicycles like Monark in Sweden and Tunturipyörä in Finland. The two types resembled each other as well. 'The exercise bicycle has a saddle, pedals and handlebars as the common bike, but by means of the pedals a kind of resistant flywheel with a brake is made to rotate' (Skott 1986, p.15).

The Sport Museum of Finland has a collection of three exercise cycles, and they are all only slight modifications of a usual bicycle. Originally they came from Holland and Germany. They are made of steel and their wheels are supported by a frame. Until the end of the 1960s the exercise cycles were similar, modified bicycles (figure 38).

The Swedish firm Monark-Crescent arranged a design competition in 1968 to promote new solutions for fitness exercise equipment in the home. One of the awards was given to a cabinet model which included a folding bicycle (Form 1968, p.586). From the beginning of the 1980s on, new kinds of exercise cycles have been designed (appendix 4). In brochures and advertisements the cycles have been depicted in staged environments. Only a few pictures have been taken in homes. Even then the cycle was placed in a large plain bedroom or bathroom with only a few other pieces of furniture (Design 1988; Talouselämä 1992).

Figure 38. An exercise cycle from the late 1960s (Form 1967, p.491).

The Finnish company Tunturi Oy has introduced a divergent exercise cycle, the E 450. The design has received an award and has been introduced as an example of new successful design in Finland (Design Forum 1992, p.4; Talouselämä 1992; Tirkkonen 1993, p.82). The competitive edge on the market is a new design and not a new technical innovation. The model E 450 was developed for an advanced but non-professional trainer (figure 39). It belongs to the product line called the 'Active Line' for both homes and training centres. The technical and ergonomic aspects of the exercise cycle are presented in appendix 4.

The model E 450 as a sign

The overall form of the cycle can be visually divided into parts and corresponding colours, such as the saddle, the gray frame, the white bottom, the handlebars, the flywheel, the pedals, and the back support (under the flywheel). The composition of the cycle can be divided vertically into only two main parts as well (i.e., the frame and the saddle and the handlebars with their supportive rod). The two diagonally rising rods (for the saddle and the handlebars) form a dynamic and expressive composition.

The exercise cycle is easy to approach in a natural way because many people have experienced the bike and because the two have many details in common.

Especially the saddle, the rods for the saddle and handlebars, the pedals, and the flywheel are reminders of the cycle's origin and tradition. Compared with other models of cycles on the market, the E 450 resembles a normal bicycle less because of its divergent overall design. The flywheel at the back of the cycle and its smooth form distinguishes it radically from other cycles.

The colour of the cycle as an iconic sign seems to vary according to its surroundings. In a bright illuminated training centre the cycle seems to accommodate itself well to a clean and tidy environment, as well as to other equipment mainly of the same colouration. In a bicycle shop, however, it seems to fit with colourful leisure-time equipment only through its colourful details. On the whole, the white cycle deviates from the bicycles and bicycle equipment in the shop. In the sports section of a department store it fits in better because of the light white surfaces of the surroundings (white walls, ceilings and floor). It seems to fit better with the room than with the other equipment in the section.

When the cycle's expressivity and metaphorical reference is examined, it seems like it might be a water bird, for example. The saddle and its rod resemble the head and neck, the flywheel its tail, the pedals its webbed feet. The expression of the saddle as a

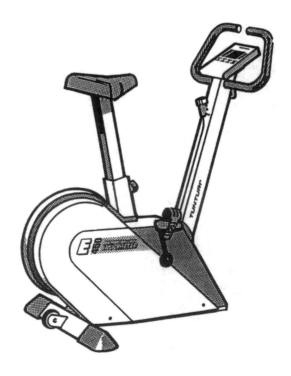

Figure 39. Model E 450 by Tunturipyörä Oy.

head looks snub-nosed, self-confident and self-respecting. Such a metaphorical interpretation is not just play for its own sake, but it can be of help when an object's characteristics are interpreted.

The handlebars look like curved horns from the front, and thus the cycle looks like a horned being with corresponding expressivity. The handlebars have circular yellow dots like eyes. They are visually active parts with tension towards other parts. The horisontal back support (under the flywheel) has gray parts of rubber like paws, as they are called. The plastic coating of the handlebars is soft and skin-like.

The cycle has a style made for the company's product line; it has a 'Tunturi' style. The E 450 model is part of a fairly coherent line emphasized by graphic design. In training centres in Helsinki (Kuntorivakka, Solana Fitness, SVUL), as well as in brochures and advertisements, the style characteristic for such centres and their equipment can be distinguished. The room and equipment are designed in this style to create an atmosphere. The style can be called sporty or the fitness exercise style. Furthermore, it may remind a person of careless, easy living with references to holidays and leisure time in the summer. In a training centre the cycle also looks like a technical appliance. Thus one can question how the (technical) appliance fits the home milieu.

The cycle seems to be an iconic index in many ways (many details) because of the similarities between its parts and bodily parts, as can be recognized from the direction of the form. The body rests on the saddle, the handlebars and the pedals. These cycle parts are like extensions of the body from the point of view of design. At the same time they direct attention and guide the actions of getting on the cycle.

The telephone kiosk

The third example differs from the two previous ones in its use, location, construction and measurement. The kiosk has attained attention in design publications (Industrial Design 1960, p.48; Design 152, 1961, p.63; Design 158, 1962, p.73; Form 1971, p.78 and p.79; form 72, 1975, p.9; Hufnagl 1981; Industrial Design 1984, p.55; form 133, 1991, p.70; Blueprint 1991), and it has been the subject of design competitions in many countries. A kiosk has been a popular exercise in design education also (Industrial Design 1962, p.42; Design 395, 1981, p.50; Form 7, 1986, p.40; Sotamaa 1987, p.68; Design 500, 1990, p.16).

The kiosk is considered to be both a design product and an architectural product, an object of interest to both designers and architects, which increases its interest for semantic analysis. The design of a kiosk includes the planning of the inner room, as well as the planning of its location outdoors in a public environment and of its elements as a form of architecture. These features differ from usual product design.

The history of the telephone kiosk has been multiphased and interesting from the design point of view. In the 1880s in England private telephone companies set up telephone services for the public in busy places like railway stations, hotels and shops. At the turn of the century, the companies started to construct separate kiosks outdoors to make the use of a telephone easier. Most of these early kiosks were wooden sentry boxes or of the road-mender's type, but there was little uniformity. Different companies erected different types of boxes, while the local authorities insisted on special designs in harmony with their surroundings (Stamp 1989, p.3). After World War I, the General Post Office (GPO) in England started to standardize the kiosks. The initiative of the GPO was an improved version of the wooden sentry box, the kiosk K 1. Its production was started in 1923, and eleven years later in 1934 there were 6 300 of them in use. Today however there are only a few. Aesthetically, the K 1 was not a success.

K 2

The recently established Royal Fine Art Commission (1924) organized a competition in England and invited three architects to participate. The Commission conceived the architect as the best person to design what was, in fact, more like a miniature building than an ornamented sentry box (Stamp 1989, p.6 and 10). The organizer recommended an iron construction and estimated a prize for it. As a result of this competition Sir Giles Gilbert Scott's well-known red kiosk, later the K 2, came into being (figure 40). The original design of Scott was, however, a kiosk in silver gray. Inside it was greenish blue. The wooden door was made of teak.

The K 2 was set up and positioned in the streets from 1926 on. The original wooden prototype was re-erected in London within the entrance colonnades of the Burlington House off Piccadilly square and is still in use (Stamp 1989, p.11). The form is classic, and more than a utilitarian structure. The impression is based on the carefully worked details, and the form rising from a podium to a pediment; it has a monumental presence. Its overall form is coherent. Such a form could cause discordance with its

Figure 40. The K 2. The perforated crown figure shows that the kiosk is state property. At the same time it serves ventilation. The writing 'Telephone' is on a glass plate through which the light from inside shines out in the dark.

surroundings of another style. The strong character of the K 2 seems, however, to have a positive effect. The kiosk is conceived as pleasing, and it has been valued as a neighbouring building. Its adaptability to various environments has not been criticized.

In 1935, eleven years after the design of the K 2, Scott was asked to design a new kiosk, which was later called the K 6 (the 'Jubilee'). It is a smaller and slenderer model than the K 2. It has some typically modernistic features like the horisontal composition of the door glass. The red colour (in accordance with the 'Post Office red') was an important factor for the success of the kiosk, although the use of a more discrete colour as a shade of light gray was thought to fit some areas of great natural beauty better. This is the famous red English kiosk.

At the same time wooden sentry box like kiosks were also set up by motoring organizations (Stamp 1989, p.16).

In 1959 the GPO in England asked a young architect, Nevil Conder, to design a new kiosk, which later became the K 7 (Gray 1959; Design 173, 1963, p.47). Before this initiative the GPO had consulted the most important art and design organizations, like the Council of Industrial Design, The Royal Fine Art Commission and the Royal Fine Arts Commission of Scotland. K 7 was made of aluminium and glass. According to Stamp (1989, p.18), a critic in favour of the old Scott model, 'here was the new aesthetic: light, rectilinear and insubstantial'. Instead of being monumental it was transparent. It was surely new in appearance, comparable with the Swedish telephone kiosk designed by Axel Acking in 1955 (Form 1955, p.190). Again in 1965 a competition of kiosk designs was organized in England. Three designers were invited to participate and as a result the successful K 8 was developed. It was a modern red kiosk, again in cast iron.

In the Unites States the telephone company Bell and the well-known design consultant Henry Dreyfuss started to apply ergonomics in their design of a kiosk. This collaboration took place as late as the 1960s although they had been partners for already 35 years (Conway 1965, p.59). As a result of their cooperation a new model was launched; it is illustrated in figure 41.

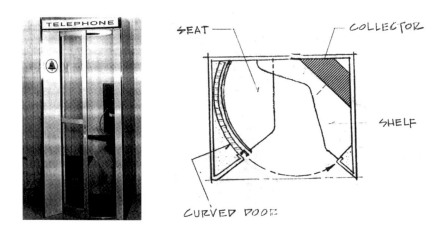

Figure 41. The design by Dreyfuss in aluminium and glass.

In the 1960s also kiosks in steel and fibreglass were made in the United States (Industrial Design 1960, p.48; Design 158, 1962, p.73). Many other countries, like Holland, Germany, Switzerland and Denmark, have been organizing design competitions as well (form 133, 1991, p.70; Design 518, 1992, p.53).

When the British Telecom was separated from the GPO in 1984, all of the kiosks were replaced by American kiosks as a result of the reorganization. These new kiosks were designed to last for 15 years, while the earlier kiosks were thought to last for at least 50 years. The K 2 by Scott has lasted even longer in use. The hurry to introduce new models was explained in terms of corporate identity and business economics.

Stamp (1989) found a tragic element in the development of the British telephone kiosk. New models were introduced also in 1988, but they were conceived as kitsch and commercial. According to Stamp, these new kiosks cannot actually

128

be compared with the old model K 2 because they represent another way of thinking. (See also Design 437, 1985, p.15 and Design 502, 1990, p.68.) The cultural and artistic civilization is disappearing.

The debate about kiosks in England may have influenced discussions in other countries. The many phases and rapid sequences in the history of the kiosk draws my attention to following the British development. It seems difficult to find sensible reasons for this kind of design activity. The kiosk has changed from a massive and distinct form to a transparent construction elsewhere as well. Examples of such a shift could be seen in the Public Design exhibition in Frankfurt in 1989 (Design 492, 1989, p.17). A characteristic form has been conceived to fit in well with different urban milieus, whereas plain and more transparent designs are disapproved of. A product like the K 2 draws attention to itself and is not conceived as part of the environment. In addition, it can function as an interesting sign. A simple transparent kiosk may seem more demanding and the quality of its surroundings gets attention. Its place requires, then, special care.

The Danish design competition on telephone kiosks arranged in the 1980–1981 has been exceptionally well documented (Bernsen 1985). The aim was to find a better option for the old green kiosk in steel and for the other models on the market. An ideal for the design was an open street screen. The measurement should cover a range from the size of a 10-year-old child upwards. In addition to the technical and ergonomic requirements the competition programme emphasized the signal character of the kiosk. It should also fit in various urban environments unpretentiously (figure 42) and, at the same time, have a character of its own. Its appearance should be comparable with the easily recognizable typeforms such as the fire plug or the pillar box. Last but not least, it was to express the high quality of the telephone company's services and function as a symbol of Copenhagen. The winning design was set up on the Townhall Square and three other central places in the city, and it was inaugurated by the Mayor on 23 May 1984.

129

Miljørigtig

Der er udskrevet konkurrence om nye københavnske telefonbokse, og betingelsen er, at de skal passe naturligt ind i ethvert gadebillede.

Figure 42. A cartoon about a kiosk's environmental adaptation (Bernsen 1985, p.45).

The German post office Bundespost organized a design competition in 1978 concerning a telephone kiosk with especially the wheelchair user in mind (form 85, 1979, p.12; form 92, 1980, p.56). The winning design was an octagonal yellow kiosk which best fit the range of previous kiosks. It was mainly valued for its ergonomic features. Yellow, especially corn yellow, had earlier been chosen as a symbol of the German post office because it is considered the traditional colour of the post and more easily recognized than its graphic figures such as the horn (Weidemann 1978). The results of tests of animal behaviour (with bright yellow) supported the decision. Bright yellow was the most efficient colour in signalizing. Cultural connections of yellow influenced, too. Yellow has been conceived as referring to forward movement, progress, modernity, future and hope. The colour was regarded the most important detail of the visual image of the post.

130

In 1986, eight years later, the German post office arranged another design competition (form 115, p.52). The aim was a transparent telephone kiosk which would adapt itself to different environments. It was to be protective against climatic conditions and vandalism and both technically and economically functional. The winning model was a plain transparent construction. The second prize was given to a design by Richard Sapper (figure 43). The joyful expression was praised, but it was not conceived as an acceptable form for a modern public service institution.

Figure 43. Richard Sapper's entry to the kiosk design competition.

What happened in Finland?

A telephone company was established in Helsinki in 1882. At the same time the idea of inserting coins for operation was put into practice, and during the summer the first public telephone was set up in A. A. F. Lindberg's tobacco shop in Helsinki (Turpeinen 1981, p.517). The first outdoor telephones appeared in Helsinki in 1912 (colour page 3).

In the 1930s, kiosks were made of concrete and steel and painted green. Th. Bruun, an architect, designed a steel kiosk which was painted green and which was set up in the city from 1932 on (Suomen Kuvalehti 1932, p.1309). From the 1960s on the usual materials have been aluminium and glass. In Finland, as in many other countries, a kiosk especially for wheelchair users has been set up since the 1980s.

There were about 500 telephone kiosks in Helsinki in 1993. As an alternative, there are also nowadays telephone booths set up in covered urban spaces. There have been critical discussions about telephone kiosk design also in Finland (Carlson 1988, p.40–44). In her broad survey on street furniture Ulla-Kirsti Junttila (1978, p.9 and 1986, p.124) described the telephone kiosk in Helsinki as a tower-like technical construction. (See figure 44.) She especially accepted the green colour, which fits well in an urban environment. A green kiosk looks home-like and adapts itself especially in older parts of the city. The green colour makes

Figure 44. Telephone kiosks in Helsinki in the 1970s and early 1980s. On the left a green model and on the right a gray model.

it look slender too. The gray aluminium kiosk in Helsinki, on the other hand, looks unconnected from its surroundings and is technically cool. Therefore, it seems better suited for new areas.

The kiosk model m-89

The choice of model for the kiosk was easy because the city of Helsinki had just launched a new product called m-89 (see colour page 3). Eventually the new model will replace most of the older ones in the city.

The model m-89 has been set up in Helsinki since 1989, and it has been designed in several variations such as a double, a large version especially for wheelchair users, and a wall version. The new model received critical comments in the main newspaper just after its introduction (figure 45).

Aikansa karu kuva

PUHELINKIOSKI ON julkisista julkisin rakennus. Esimerkiksi Helsingin Puhelinyhdistyksen toimialueella näitä palvelupisteitä on 730. Kioskien ulkoinen muoto on vuosikymmenten varrella muuttunut, kutakin aikaa ja kehitystä kuvaten. Ensi vuonna katukuvaan tulee taas uusi kioskityyppi.

Kun vuosisatamme alun puhelinkioskia verrataan tähän uusimpaan kioskiin, voidaan tehdä johtopäätöksiä suomalaisen arkkitehtuurin kehityksestä. Käsitykset muodon kauneudesta ovat pitkällä aikavälillä tietysti muuttuneet, mutta näinkö paljon? Kysymykseen voi vastata kuka vain, koska se on makuasia.

Toinen kehityssuunta on vakavampi. Vuosisadan alun kioskisuunnittelija näyttää pitäneen lähtökohtana romanttista silmäniloa, pehmeää muotoa, koristeellisuutta. Nykypäivän arkkitehti joutui etsimään ratkaisua, joka parhaiten kestää ilkivallan. Olemme siis niin murheellisessa tilanteessa, että on elettävä vandalismin ehdoilla.

Figure 45. Editorial of the biggest newspaper in Finland, the Helsingin Sanomat, in 1989, is headed The austere image of its time.

133

The technical and ergonomic factors of the model m-89 can be found in appendix 5. In a Finnish design magazine, the kiosk form m-89 was compared with an older model (Herler 1989, p.37). (Compare with Stamp 1989.) Both kiosk forms were 'anthropomorphized'.

Accordingly, the older model looked upright, harmonious, like a man with dignity, standing like a watchful servant well aware if his function. The new model was barelegged under its coat with a flattened cap on its head. The reason given for their divergent appearances were the different proportions of the kiosks.

The kiosk m-89 as a sign

Standing on a street corner, the kiosk looks like a distinct product. It is a transparent slender green metal construction and rectangular like a box. A ceiling lamp is lit. The kiosk does not seem to assimilate with other products in the street or merge into the townscape. It deviates from them as a new and tidy product with a specific colour. The other objects in the neighbourhood are usually older and shabby technical products or colourful kiosks for other purposes, like flowers and candy, or stands for outdoor advertising or bus stops.

Its green colour stands out, but, at the same time, it adjusts itself to the facades of surrounding buildings and shop windows and to the vegetation. Set up in a park, its special blueish shade of green can be distinguished.

The rectangular glass box-like form is outlined by dark green horisontal and vertical laths. They make the kiosk look somewhat striped. The light glassy impression is emphasized by the thin metal pegs in the bottom corners. The pegs seem to lift it up from the ground. The form tradition of the telephone kiosk is an upright tower and rectangular box. Due to its traditional form and the windows it is fairly easy to perceive as a telephone kiosk. The model m-89 is plain and neutral, but still, in my view, it cannot be considered inexpressive or dull.

134

The kiosk has a facade and a back. The green colour plate is the back side, and therefore the kiosk looks closed and turning away when seen from the back. The door is noted because of the gray handle, and the entrance is emphasized by a peak in the front part of the ceiling and a step in front at the base. The asymmetric form of the handle does not show where to grasp to open the door. But the form may help a person to remember the function.

Traces of use can be noted even in new kiosks. Trash and dirt pile up on the floor and in the front of the kiosk. The inside also becomes damaged (the table plate is broken) and areas are filled with graffity, mainly tags.

The ceiling lamp is signalling and looks welcoming. It even resembles a cosy indoor light, which gives the kiosk a sympathetic warm character, even though the real temperature in winter may be very cold. The kiosk does not look cold, and there is a conflict between the appearance and the real experience. The metal handle can feel ice cold as well.

The kiosk m-89 was designed on a commission of the City of Helsinki, and this is the reason for its green colour. The colour connects it to the kiosk tradition and to other street furniture in Helsinki, like the bus stops, benches and garbage cans. The green colour creates uniformity even if the shade varies.

The bicycle helmet

The fourth example differs from the other three because it is a piece of equipment to be worn. From a design point of view it is problematic because it is close to the body as a garment, and as such it can be perceived as part of a person's clothing or dress. On the other hand, it can be looked upon as a separate piece of equipment, belonging to the bicycle and cycling. As a product its design is on the traditional borderline of fashion and clothing design and industrial design and is confronted with the limits of both fields. Therefore, its analysis might bring new aspects to a semantic analysis.

Compared with the other three examples in my study the helmet does not have a complex and long history of form. It is a new product. Finnish literature about cycling in general deals briefly with equipment and accessories like the cap and the protective helmet (Skott 1986, p.122). The traditional protective headgear in leather protected against rub injuries. It has been obligatory in amateur competitions. The cap, among other equipment such as cyclists' trousers, shirts, and bottles, is mentioned to have a protective function against too much sunshine and 'the cap has become a common characteristic for bicyclists in the whole world. Hardly any cyclist wants to be without a cap' (Kempas and Pajunen 1987).

The bicycle helmet can be compared with helmets designed for other protective purposes (e.g., building workers' helmets, ice hockey helmets, baseball helmets, etc.).

When Nordlund and Sitari (1989) wrote their research-based article about children's bicycles in Finland, they analysed the bicycle and some other equipment. They only briefly mentioned the helmet, although the aim of the article was to attract attention to the great number of children's accidents with bicycles. Earlier in a similar article the helmet had not been mentioned at all (Lehtonen 1986). Since the beginning of the 1980s, helmets have been designed especially for children, and they have been tested. But they still have many shortcomings.

There are many different models of bicycle helmets on the market (appendix 6). Among them are also models which do not fulfil the requirements for protection (Lundgren 1983; Puomila 1993).

A protective piece of equipment or an accessory?

Most of the injuries of bicyclists concern the head (Farm 1982, Thompson et al. 1989; Thompson et al.1990a; Thompson et al. 1990b; Koivurova 1993). The severest ones are also head injuries. In the Helsinki area, one-third of brain injuries concern bicyclists (Seppälä and Juvela 1991). Many countries have organized campaigns to increase the use of protective helmets (DiGuiseppi et al. 1989; Olkkonen and Koivurova 1990; Bliar 1991; Runyan and Runyan 1991; Hjelte 1993; Farm 1994). Their efficiency has been discussed, as well as the effects on the national economy (Hanley 1991; Koivurova 1993, p.11). A comparison with the seat belt in a car has been made in Australia, and, accordingly, the helmet has been obligatory there since 1990 (McDermott 1991).

Literature on a cyclist's helmet is mainly concerned with its protective features and the cyclist's safety. Problems of appearance or taste are mentioned only incidentally. For those who emphasize protective aspects, the question of how to get people to use a helmet is critical. The problem seems to be how to get people to use a helmet in spite of its labelling and uncomfortable features. The protective aspect does not suffice.

In advertising the helmet is combined with a sporty achievement and, on the other hand, with other bicycle equipment. The helmet looks therefore more like an elegant accessory than like a protective item. In brochures (1993) adult cyclists wear caps, while children have helmets. The children's models differ from those worn by sportsmen.

The cyclist's helmet deviates from helmets worn in other sports like ice hockey and football. It is merely part of the protective dressing in these sports. Similarly, in many other sports, helmets belong to the clothing. Helmets are primarily protective items, even though they have decorations, figures, letters and colour patches added to them.

The choice of a model for analysis seemed at first arbitrary. There were models similar to those of bicycle racers on the market, as well as hat-like models and models for children. I selected a model which was as close as possible to the recommendations of the Finnish Society of Traffic Safety (Liikenneturva 1992, Koivurova 1993). A model called Skymaster by the well-known Italian company MET seemed to fulfil the recommendations (colour page 4).

Technical and ergonomic data on the MET Skymaster helmet can be found in appendix 6.

The Skymaster helmet as a sign

When this new product is picked up from its package, it looks fine and shiny. A bright colouring increases the impression. When put on the head it looks like a hat or a cap or a shell. Its form makes the head look larger. The head looks out of proportion with the rest of the body. Perhaps this is one of the reasons for a helmet's negative connotations, which may label its wearer. People easily pay attention to proportional deviations of the body and attach qualities like misfit, clumsiness and slow motion to the form.

The helmets on the market today have a strikingly similar form and style. This similarity may reduce the use of the helmet, if it is worn as an accessory and part of one's outfit. The Skymaster model looks aerodynamic (supporting fast moving) and sporty. This impression is increased by bright red tapes on both sides, which look like stripes of speed familiar from comic books. The tapes look like stylized M-letters as well and can refer to the company MET. The chin strap makes the helmet look like an appliance.

The Skymaster has a positive expression on the basis of its colours as iconic signs. It can be associated with bright colours in advertising and graphics of sports equipment, which, in turn, have been displayed in cheerful leisure-time contexts in advertising.

The colour of the Skymaster can also be linked to the colour of traffic signals and the work environment (neon orange). It can be seen as a warning colour signal. The colourful appearance and the neon shade of orange may also refer to cheap mass products of low quality. It can be associated with plastic knicknacks and with banal sales posters on market places.

The rim of the Skymaster has indentations on both sides for the ears. Together with the tip of the helmet in the front they point at the helmet's position on the head. When compared with other models, the helmet seems hat-like, which is characteristic for the Skymaster model. When looking at some other models, a person cannot easily distinguish the front of the helmet from the back. They lack pointing indices.

Summary of the four examples as signs

The steam irons, the exercise cycle, and the telephone kiosk functioned in 13 different ways as signs. The bicycle helmet showed 12 modes of sign functioning (table 1). All four product examples had the same quantity of references as iconic and indexical signs. The telephone kiosk had fewer references as an iconic sign than the other three examples, but one more indexical reference. Symbolic references were fewer in quantity.

The references of the steam irons were more indexical (6 modes) than iconic or symbolic. The emphasis was similar with the references of the telephone kiosk (7 modes). The exercise cycle mainly had references as an iconic sign (6 modes), whereas the bicycle helmet had an equal number of iconic sign references and indexical references (5 modes). The products had no symbolic references deriving from their position, posture or material. This result cannot be seen as a failure of the grouping of the references because it aimed at presenting a broad list of possibilities for interpretation. Rather the result shows that some design products do not function as signs in every possibly conceivable way in the list. The lack of symbolic positions and materials can be a cultural feature as well, and it would be too hasty to consider it a shortcoming of the examples.

Although the number of summarized sign references was almost equal for the different products, their distribution according to mode varied. The emphasis on iconic, indexical or symbolic sign functioning varied. Both the summary and distribution are interesting because it can be concluded that a common everyday product functions as a sign in many different ways (12 and 13 modes). The character of the different products is also illuminated. It can be described by looking at the distribution of the references according to iconic, indexical and symbolic accentuation.

In addition to the quantity and distribution of the various sign functions, it is interesting to examine how they affect the interpretation of each product. Looking at the quantity of modes reveals the variation of the references and interpretation, but does not allow the content of the reference to be dealt with. The iconic function (form tradition, style, metaphor) seemed to dominate in the interpretation of the products. In the interpretation of the plain telephone kiosk even very slight indices seemed to attract attention, like the handle, the peak of the roof, the step in front, small traces of use and the like. The many symbolic signs of the steam irons seemed to characterize them. Even the symbolic signs functioned in a dominant way if there were several of them.

Form tradition, metaphor, style, pointing signs, traces, touch of material and the company's markings seemed to be especially applicable modes in interpreting the product examples. All of the products had such sign functioning.

In table 1 the quantity of the different modes of sign functioning has been summarized.

The product examples as iconic signs

The products seemed to refer as iconic signs through their form as a whole, their colour and some of their details. All of the products referred to previous models and a form tradition. Especially the steam iron, the exercise cycle and the kiosk embodied such references. A new product like the cyclist's helmet had almost no

iconic signs	irons	cycle	kiosk	helmet	No.
1. tradition	x	x	x	x	4
2. colour	x	x	-	x	3
3. material	-	x	-	x	2
4. metaphor	x	x	x	x	4
5. style	x	x	x	x	4
6. environment	x	x	-	-	2
	5	6	3	5	

indexical signs	irons	cycle	kiosk	helmet	No.
1. tool	x	x	-	-	2
2. direction	x	x	x	x	4
3. use	new	-	x	new	1
4. trace	x	x	x	x	4
5. signals	-	-	x	-	1
6. noise	x	-	x	x	3
7. smell	-	-	-	x	1
8. touch	x	x	x	x	4
9. markings	x	x	x	-	3
	6	5	7	5	

symbolic signs	irons	cycle	kiosk	helmet	No.
1. graphics	x	x	x	x	4
2. colour	-	x	x	x	3
3. form	x	-	-	-	1
4. position	-	-	-	-	
5. material	-	-	-	-	
	2	2	2	2	
	13	13	13	12	

Table 1. The quantity and distribution of the (clusters of) modes of sign functions in the interpretation of the product examples.

resemblance to previous helmets in other contexts, such as those of soldiers or sportsmen.

With the help of iconic references an attempt can be made to show traditional features and new features that have not appeared before. All of the products had been redesigned in the 1980s and had been given new characteristics that deviated from their tradition. All of the products showed a trend towards something new, a new form detached from tradition. This trend can be seen simultaneously since some traditional details of the product remain. However, the result is not always an equal balance between new and traditional characteristics. Rather, one of them seems to dominate the other and affect the interpretation. A new form may include merely a hint of a traditional feature, like some models of the steam iron. An example would be the dark border referring to the iron as a traditionally heavy tool. As a sign it may further connote durability and trust in use and then be considered a better tool than the other irons. The other irons, the smooth wholly white ones, look feeble beside it.

Many details of the steam irons refer to durability and long life-span. However, consumers cannot easily get acquainted with the technical functions if they want. Most steam irons cannot be repaired and maintained in homes at all.

A trend opposite the traditional expression can be outlined as well. It involves developing an even smoother product. A smooth white form connects the iron to other forms of household appliances of the 1980s. They look clean and easy to use. An iron in another colour could look old-fashioned among them. What is

Figure 46. A new steam iron, the Tefal Ultragliss 20.

142

more important, they may not look as clean. The design of a smooth steam iron has been even more emphasized in some new models of the 1990s. These models refer to speed and less work load even more effectively than before. Ironing seems easy and fast (figure 46).

On the basis of their size and functions, the handy traveller's iron relates to temporary use. It seems to be technically simple, having a weaker performance. It refers to leisure-time and sports equipment through its colours, rather than to household appliances.

Ironing may be even made to look like a leisure-time activity, avoiding an image of a boring duty or a tiring everyday effort. Such a utensil no longer looks like an ordinary tool. The colours of its details are important features that affect the interpretation as, for example, the pastel shades of the controls and the water tank. The new shade of turquoise may refer to sea water on a sunny summer day. For example, the water tank colour may be an emphasized detail of the design and the product may have been given the name Aqua or Azur to support the impression.

Such references of steam irons are iconic sign functions, and they play a role when products are compared because their characteristics appear more clearly. A similar discussion is also relevant for the exercise cycle, the kiosk and the helmet. Looking at a thing as an iconic sign can help define features of style and name its style. This process can be useful in design. When designers have analysed a thing as an iconic sign, they might think of developing or changing the style. 'Style' now has a broader meaning and does not limit itself to established features. Design becomes more deliberate and possibly more successful when alternative iconic references have been weighed. Designers pay attention to a larger context with the help of the interpreted references and do not focus on the concrete product only. This outlook may be beneficial when a design object (the product) is seen in a surrounding, in a context where it is used.

Cycling as a sport and the helmets used by racers have been models for cyclists' helmets designed for everyday use. Other sports accessories may have influenced the design, too. Sporty features are borrowed for helmets used in other contexts, like daily cycling on the way to work and leisure-time cycling in the countryside. Sports helmets are like master products that lend their colours and graphics and form a style. Common adjectives are sporty, lightweight, fast, efficient, casual, tidy. The design of my example seemed to aim at making both the product and the user look impressive. These qualities were emphasized by the design. Many signs seemed to function together in this direction. For example, the logotype of the company had been adjusted to the overall style. Other trends in the designs were not apparent.

I conceived features of style as iconic sign functions because the forms within a style are related with the help of visual similarity. For example, the telephone kiosk can be seen as a fragile glass box. It is a plain construction, but it is not inexpressive. It has an original expressivity of its own because it is, at the same time, clearly distinct, mirroring the environment. In addition, the environment is seen through it. Thus the environment lends its qualities to the glassy box, which changes accordingly. Of course this distinct green box-like construction is simultaneously conceived as having a specific practical function.

I aimed at a coherent application in my analyses of sign functions. However, it is not always easy to decide the group to which a reference belongs. For example, the iconic and symbolic signs often seem to merge into iconic symbols, as in the case of the control button in figure 47.

When grouping the iconic signs, I emphasized resemblance of forms and not a conventional meaning of the sign. An iconic symbol is a sign with conventional meaning in which the reference R–O is emphasized by resemblance. The cloud symbol is a common example of such a sign function for irons. The symbol on the spray button also functions as an iconic sign when it resembles a water spray.

Figure 47. A cloud pictured in the steam button of an iron.

An indexical sign can also include iconic signs, as can be seen in figure 47. The rays indicate a spray (as an index) because the button is actually connected to the water spray and the lines show the direction of the spray as well. The reference includes an actual connection, although the water does not come out exactly from the figure itself, but by pushing the button.

Why, then, should the cloud figure be an iconic symbol and the spray figure an index? The cloud on the steam button has a tangible connection to outcoming steam when pushed. Both of these figures require an understanding of a conventional meaning. To give a relevant interpretation to the rays on the button, a person must know the convention (i.e., the symbol). It seems that both of these figures are first symbols and only second are they iconic and indexical references. Therefore, I have grouped them both among the symbolic modes of references.

When designers design products, they design sign functions as well. Sign functions should be given particular attention, and they should be changed if needed. Symbols are not, however, easily transformed because their meaning may be rooted in conventional agreement over a long period of time. This tradition does not mean that knowledge of symbolic meaning should be less important to a designer than the other sign functions.

Signs functions differ. The typical characteristic for iconic signs is a subjective interpretation. Design cannot control it. The symbol is a more stable interpretation as a 'cultural unit', as Eco would call it. For example, the signs of the exercise cycle and the telephone kiosk may be either iconic or symbolic, or a combination of both. By distinguishing between the two, I am trying to show how the product functions as a sign and the emphasis in the functioning: resemblance or agreement. Only then can I continue to discuss the content of the references, which is the content in the relation R–O and the meaning in the interpretation R–I.

The examples should be analysed in the context of their use, where they seem to belong, in a 'semantic field' as Eco points out (1979, p.83). The context should be known in advance. An iron can be interpreted as a household item at a certain time (here 1989–1994), an exercise cycle as a piece of training and fitness equipment, and a telephone kiosk as street furniture. Cyclist's helmets seem to have two dominant frames of reference: protective sports equipment and outdoor dress in general (as hats). As signs they seem to belong to the first group. The exercise cycle may have a frame of reference in a home milieu also. It can be seen as part of the furniture in a home. This quality was mentioned among the requirements for its new design, but was not expressed in its sign functioning.

Colour as an iconic sign of a product is important. Colour needs to be deliberately designed as it seems to have a strong influence on sign functioning. Colour can even be a limiting factor of design. For example, the cycle seemed hygienic, easy to maintain and lightweight. Black exercise cycles are made with other references accordingly. Compared with the commoner white products, they seem heavy and powerful as if their heaviness would better suit the activity they are made for (i.e., training and conditioning one's body, which can be demanding heavy work). The black colour could possibly refer to a masculine product and be aimed at appealing to men better. Many products on the market aimed at masculine users, like machines, hand tools and items emphasizing technical function, are often black or dark coloured. A black cycle may relate to these as iconic signs.

The metaphors of a product can function as dominant signs for a long period. Thus they define the expression and 'character' of a product. Common metaphors in my analysis were, among others, the references to human and animal bodily parts, such as the face, neck and feet of a being. For example, an American cyclist's helmet has been given a new design with emphasized iconic sign functioning. The designer saw the prototype version first as something 'rodentlike, then snakelike – the mouth suggested the Chrysler Viper show car. But . . . what it most resembled was a fish – an aggressive fish' (Patton 1994, p.66). Therefore, the designer accentuated the resemblance with a pair of teeth in the front opening and moulded scales on the hard shell as well.

All four example products had signs pointing to their use and technical aspects. The controls pointed in a direction with the help of grooves and arrows. Indices can show how to use a product and how to wear it. They also indicate the facade. An index may be a reminder of a particular use of a product.

The irons and the helmet were analysed as new products, but the cycle and the kiosk were products already in use during the analysis. Traces of use can be interpreted as cultural signs, which show abrasion, dirt, level of tidiness, patina, and the need for maintenance, mending and repair. An analysis of the traces of use as signs seems to me an interesting topic, but it will require another, different type of material.

Light signals were indexical signs on steam irons. The light inside the kiosk can also be interpreted as indicating a place which really functions. The noise of a product may indicate temporary use or technical function. Such indices are apparent in use, like the click of the lock of the helmet's chin strap, the creak and slam of the opening and closing door of the kiosk or the whizzing of the spray when the water tank of an iron is emptied.

The indices of touch were mainly connected to controls and handles. In addition, pedals, the saddle, the (stuffing) inside the hard shell helmet and the chin strap cause sense impression through touching. The temperature of the materials in touching are indexical signs, too. These features inform about the material and refer to methods of production. Important characteristics with regard to the sense of touch may show an attitude towards the product. A person can conclude how much effort is spent on the finishing, for example. Unpolished, uneven, rough, defective points of contact can be interpreted as a sign of a cheap product. An iconic sign (e.g., a feature of style seen in relation to markings of a production tool) may influence a person's conception of the product's value.

My examples showed traces of production such as casting seams and unevenness of moulds, welding seams and methods of colouring.

The exercise cycle, the telephone kiosk and the bicycle helmet had only a few symbols. The irons had many. This does not necessarily mean, however, that the symbols were less important signs than the others. For example, the symbolic green colour of the telephone kiosk was a dominant feature of representation. The controls often had a symbolic reference included in their material appearance. Accordingly, a product with many controls may have many symbols as well.

The logotype of the manufacturing company is added to the product as a distinct mark. The irons and the kiosk also had other symbolic figures and informative devices such as regulations and instructions of use.

A symbolic colour can be chosen by the manufacturer to connect the design to a production line. The shade of neon orange of the helmet can be regarded as a symbol in a traffic context. Then it functions as the general warning colour.

A product may function as a symbol of a particular thing, like the red K 2 kiosk designed by Scott. The kiosk has been used as a symbol of London, Britain and the British. The aim of the Danish design competition in 1985 was to create a kiosk to symbolize Copenhagen. Thus far the green telephone m–89 kiosk in

Helsinki has not functioned as a symbol of the city, and it has not yet acquired the status of a symbol.

The iron is sometimes seen as symbolizing femininity and a woman's status in a culture because it is commonly used by women and related to their domestic activities. Accordingly, it is seen as a product especially designed for the house-wife (Lupton 1993, p.18, 24–25). The advertisements of irons illustrate the work of women and also the traditional division of labour between the sexes (Giedion 1948; Hardyment 1988, Ross 1994, p.31).

Using a semantic analysis, I can define a typical product of a period in a group or a 'semantic field'. However, I do not mean a standard technical solution or a 'dominant design' (Andersson and Tushman 1990). A typical product in the semantic sense is culturally defined and close to the prototype described by Rosch (1975). It has many features in common with other products in the group and the dominant characteristics stand out. Its other features are less important, or there are only a few other notable characteristics. In the analysis of the steam irons, the Tefal seemed to represent a typical model of the late 1980s. It had a dark border at the bottom with reference to form tradition. Its iconic and symbolic sign functions did not notably differ from those interpreted for other irons. Still it was possible to distinguish the Tefal from other models because it had a distinct detail, the pastel shading of its control buttons.

A semantic analysis carried out in practice is done in phases, even though the phases cannot be sharply delineated from each other as steps. It is especially difficult to distinguish a description of the visual composition from a semantic study because, in practice, it is not possible to register the features of a composition without interpreting them as well. A product's form is perceived in connection with its interpretation, and then a meaning is related to it. A product can afford many things in many ways. Notes should be written down of different aspects at the same time. A division of the analysis into two parts seems practical, the first

to consist of data collection and orientation and the second of perception and interpretation (with the help of a checklist).

An analysis should focus on some relevant characteristics of the product to be
practical. The aim can therefore not be to collect as much data as possible about
the product and its details. Still, much knowledge is needed before a sensible
semantic study can be carried out. Data collection easily becomes a time-consuming phase that burdens the entire analysis. The data collection can be troubled
by the fact that many sources must be used because no archives exist from which
to collect data on everyday things, including their use, history, technology, production, and sales. For example, historical data must be searched for in different
museums and libraries. The Museum of Applied Art, as well as the Helsinki City
Museum, have interesting collections for the purposes of design studies. They are
complemented by special museums such as the Museum of Medical History, the
Sport Museum of Finland or the Museum of Technology.

It is difficult to know in advance precisely what kind of data will be needed for
an analysis, but, after material has been collected, it is possible to select relevant
facts and then look for more if necessary. During the data collection the appearance of topics, aspects, demands and the like recur, and this recurrence facilitates
orientation and the sorting of material. Experience in applying a semantic analysis helps, in my opinion, to estimate the material needed.

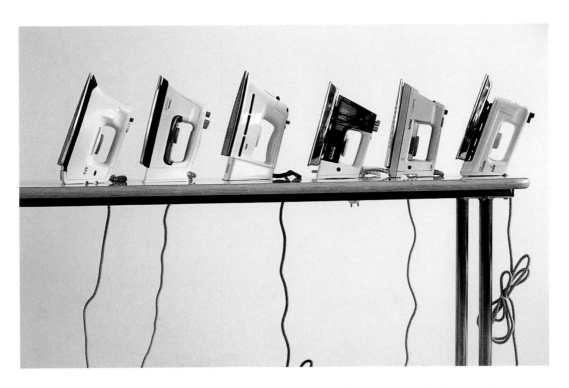

1 The steam irons in the sample material.

2   *The exercise cycle E 450. An advertisement.*

3   The telephone kiosk m-89 (right).
An old kiosk model in Helsinki from the beginning of the 20th century (above).

4   *The Skymaster helmet.*

6 AESTHETIC APPRECIATION OF PRODUCTS

An interpretation of a product's references, the semantic analysis, does not necessarily concern its aesthetics. Therefore, I wish to look closer at the aesthetics of a design product. Fundamental questions accumulate right from the start. Does the product have intrinsic aesthetic properties or should the aesthetic experience be studied? Does a person have a specific experience that can be called aesthetic? What kind of experience could it be? Is a person's experience connected with the properties of the object? How do they relate to each other?

I shall first look at the properties of the object because my study concerns products. It seems difficult to find aesthetic properties that would fit all design artefacts because they form too heterogenous a collection. An aesthetic feature of a product defined in one context may be totally missing in another, to which aesthetic features of another kind may be related (Niiniluoto 1990, p.204). For example, the colours on a banquet table can be considered aesthetic, but the same quality is not necessarily aesthetically acceptable for a table on a nature trail. Elegant details of an orchestra conductor's costume differ from those people prefer to have on a diving suit. There is no sense in trying to apply the aesthetic features of one product to another product.

The aesthetic experience has been studied by many scholars of the philosophy of art and aesthetics. They have given different explanations and their theories are conflicting. For example, R.G. Collingwood (1938, p.116) emphasizes empathy and insight into the artist's experience and feelings through the work of art. Nelson Goodman (1976), on the other hand, argues for the importance of the cognitive in aesthetic experience. Goodman does not stress the uniqueness of an aesthetic experience. The question concerning the relationship between the aesthetic experience and other kinds of experiences is interesting. How does it differ from other ways of experiencing and perceiving the world around us? What is the relationship of the aesthetic experience to the acquisition of knowledge, to logical reasoning and to memory?

Tony Bennett (1987, p.44) has illuminated these questions by connecting the aesthetic experience to the conception of reality. Accordingly, a subject has a certain kind of attitude towards reality in the first place. The aesthetic experience can be explained according to this more fundamental attitude: '. . . the aesthetic as a specific mode of the subject's mental relation to reality . . . can only be established in relation to some prior conception of the knowledge relation between subject and reality, . . ' The aesthetic experience includes then epistemological considerations, which define it. This circumstance explains why aesthetic theories vary and conflict. The French sociologist Pierre Bourdieu (1987) concludes, on the basis of vast empirical data, that the aesthetic experience is not 'pure'. It cannot be separated from ideologies and social values.

Nelson Goodman (1976, p.241–245) has included both the cognitive and the emotive in his aesthetic theory.

> This subsumption of aesthetic under cognitive excellence ... does not
> exclude the sensory or the emotive, that what we know through art is felt
> in our bones and nerves and muscles as well as grasped by our minds ...
> (Goodman 1976, p.259)

The message of this quotation seems to fit my approach as far as the work (of art), here a product, is conceived as a symbol and the aesthetic experience relates to the interpretation of a symbol. The work (of art) functions as an aesthetic symbol. Symbolization is to be judged by how well it serves the cognitive purpose in the first place. The aesthetic value depends on how well the work functions as a symbol.

In Goodman's theory (1976, p.33, 248, 258–259) the emotional experience intermingles with cognitive reasoning. The emotions function cognitively. An aesthetic experience may also increase knowledge about the world. Thus a work (of art) that succeeds in increasing knowledge is more valuable than another, less efficient in the acquisition of knowledge. The definition of the aesthetic experience now attains a strange accent, in my opinion, when the acquisition of knowledge determines the experience to such a high degree. I think that, in Goodman's theory, the efficient role of knowledge is stressed too far.

When Markus Lammenranta (1990) compared the instrumentalistic theories of the aesthetic value by Beardsley and Goodman, he noted their differences as, for example, the fact that Beardsley distinguishes between the aesthetic value and the cognitive and the moral, whereas Goodman holds that the aesthetic value is a kind of cognitive value. Then Lammenranta concluded that one of the theories must be wrong. It seems to me, however, that these theories are approaching the problem of aesthetic value in distinct ways, and, therefore, they arrive at divergent conclusions.

The starting point for Beardsley is an object that is capable of producing an aesthetic experience. The properties of the object correspond to those of the experience. Beardsley (1958, p.529) even defines the properties required of an object for an aesthetic experience. They are coherence, intensity and complexity. These properties of the object influence its (experienced) aesthetic value. Beardsley has then tried to define objective aesthetic properties, and it seems to me that this is too narrow a restriction for an approach. In the beginning of this chapter I concluded that it would not be sensible to try to find common aesthetic properties for all design products, even when regarded as very general qualities as Beardsley's are.

According to Goodman, the aesthetic properties of a product are not intrinsic, but are formed in the interpretation of the product when the product functions as a symbol. For example, the qualities of a radio, such as well-proportioned, good-shaped, in style, nice, good looking (which I call aesthetic qualities), are not only intrinsic qualities as are its size, weight and roundness, but are percepts and interpretations of the radio. When a product is conceived as a symbol, I still talk about its aesthetic properties and am aware of my interpretative relation to the product.

This relation may include both perceivable and semantic levels. The aesthetics of a product can thus be seen as part of the interpretation of a symbol. What makes a symbol an aesthetic symbol remains open.

The aesthetic can, however, be conceived in a narrower manner as an experience of pleasure. Both sides, the aesthetic as part of interpretation and the aesthetic as a sense of pleasure, are included in Aristotle's definition of the aesthetic (Tatarkiewicz 1980, p.311 and 314). The division appears also in new aesthetic literature. Alan Goldman (1990) takes both sides into consideration as well. He distinguishes between the ways of experiencing based on sense perception and those that are representational or expressive.

When Csikszentmihalyi and Rochberg-Halton (1981, p.177–178 and 182) studied everyday things in homes with the help of interviews, they also analysed the aesthetics of these things. They divided the aesthetic experience according to John Dewey into recognition and perception. The recognition of the product as merely a pleasing thing is not enough for a proper definition of an aesthetic experience. There should always be effort included in perception which enables aesthetic experience. (Compare with 'aesthetic labour' in Eco 1979, p.151–156.) Accordingly, one should not restrict the aesthetic experience to a sensual impression or reduce it to mere recognition of the conventional.

Arto Haapala (1991, p.67) defends a view of the aesthetic experience as being something appreciated as beautiful. It is a subjective and immediate experience, which is directed towards the object for its own sake. Cognitive and moral aspects are excluded from Haapala's definition of the aesthetic experience. He calls them artistic qualities instead. In this way Haapala aims at clarifying the distinct aesthetic quality in an experience. When I consider the relationship between the aesthetic and the semantic in this study, this discussion may be illuminating. The question of the limits, what is included and excluded in the aesthetic experience, seems important for further discussion.

My approach to the aesthetics of a design product could also limit itself to a study of something, which is experienced as beautiful. But it would not correspond to the questions put forth in my study. My aim is to analyse design products and interpret their representational qualities. Accordingly, I emphasize the qualities of a material object in relation to my interpretation, not in relation to a description of subjective experience or different kinds of subjective experience. However, I do not parenthesize the subjective element from my analysis of the aesthetic.

Joseph Margolis (1980, p.223) has argued for an approach in which the starting point is personal liking. One can speak of the properties of an object as filtered through one's own personal tastes and sensibilities. This thought of 'filtering' seems close to an interpretation (of references) by means of iconic signs. Thus one could think of an aesthetic icon. It would be a sign one could appreciate. In addition, in the case of iconic signs, the same kind of problem appears concerning subjectivity. Iconic signs seem subjective in the same sense as the aesthetic experience, and it cannot give up this quality without losing one of its main characteristics.

Two aspects of the aesthetic experience seem important for my further discussion, its content and its disinterested character. First, does an aesthetic experience have a content or not when defined in a narrower manner as a pleasing sense impression? What is meant by content here? If the aesthetic appreciation of a product includes the composition of colours, lines and dots only, it has no content other than this (possibly) pleasing arrangement. It has no content provided by references, which are interpretations of the arrangement. The aesthetic experience could be reduced to principles in perception psychology, like balance, dynamics and brightness.

If, on the other hand, the aesthetic experience is conceived as broader than a pleasing sense impression, one can ask if it can be disinterested (pure)? Can the object of the interpretation wholly define what is relevant in the experience (the subject then being disinterested)? Can a subject be entirely subordinated to the

A prerequisite for an aesthetic judgement is that the objects be considered in a predefined category. Then arguments can be developed for an evaluation, which is possible and sensible to discuss. The arguments are more than subjective impressions. They include more than purely perceptional properties and they relate to something. A prerequisite for a potential aesthetic experience, which could also be discussed with others, is people's awareness of a category with reasonable qualities. Only when the requirements of the category are known in advance, can one argue in a sensible way about aesthetic appreciation. The criteria are not properties of the product, such as those discussed in the beginning of this chapter, but features in a category. What could the arguments for an aesthetic appreciation of a design product be? To answer this question I continue to apply Walton's approach. In addition to perceptual properties, he presents the following two kinds of features to be considered:

a) features originating from the designer's intention: they are features that the designer wants to emphasize in the work (product) and which are meant to be taken into consideration in an evaluation;
b) features originating from the history of design and the product's own tradition.

Furthermore, Walton (1970, p.57) groups features as 'standard' to define the group as a distinct group of objects, such as the radio as a radio; 'variable' to indicate that they have nothing to do with the grouping and are thus more or less secondary; and 'contra-standard' to exclude the object from a group, such as the contra-radio features of a radio.

The three kinds of features should now be related to my approach in the semantic analysis of design products. The product is taken into consideration as a whole. As Bense (1971) already stated with good reason, the material sign vehicle is implicitly important in a design analysis. It carries out the practical purposes of a design product, not the sign. However, the conception of the product's function in this manner is too restrictive and narrow. The purpose of, for example, a bread knife would be limited to cutting bread and the purpose of a bicycle would be limited to speeding up one's movement. The evaluation of such practical and technical functions of a product is not a semantic problem, but belongs to studies of its material and syntactic dimensions and are different in nature.

When the features of, for example, a radio are analysed, one should pay attention to the designer's intentions and to the properties it was meant to have (a). In addition, features of radio design history are relevant (b). For the latter the specific radio as an object of analysis will be put in a historical context of radio designs and compared with other radios. Then the radio-like features of the radio should be analysed especially with the help of the historical aspects (b), along with its variable or secondary features, and its contra-radio features. This kind of discussion is already included in a semantic analysis, except for the designer's intention.

With the help of the aesthetic approach the analysis acquires a new feature, namely, the aspect that derives from the designer's intentions. This aspect has been discussed in the philosophy of art (e.g., Margolis 1980), and Walton (1970, p.361) points at some problems concerning this kind of information in the analysis. Intention can be vaguely and variously expressed and unclear or undiscoverable. In spite of such difficulties, I shall try to take the designer's intention into account with the help of interviews and conceive the acquired knowledge as background material for the aesthetic analysis.

The second new element brought to the semantic analysis by aesthetics is the appreciation (liking, pleasure) of the product, the question concerning its aesthetic value. If I find a product pleasing as I recognize a familiar property, it may feel like a happy reunion. It may be a remembrance or a notion, an interpretation of style. My experience then includes a semantic component. I may have recognized the reference without having localized it by naming, telling or depicting it. The pleasing aesthetic element has functioned together with an iconic sign, or, as Margolis puts it, the properties have filtered through my liking. The pleasing impression is considered in relation to other features (the semantic ones, Walton's standard, variable and contra-standard features).

The relation of something new with something familiar in an interpretation has been illuminated by Raymond Loewy from a design point of view in his book Never Leave Well Enough Alone from 1951 (Lichtenstein 1990). He took the pleasing impression into consideration as well. Loewy has formulated a principle called MAYA (most-advanced-yet-acceptable) especially to illustrate the success of a design product on the market. A successful product (that sells) is new and different and, at the same time, a familiar thing. The relation between the two qualities is flexible, and it is the designer's challenge to find the right balance. The key question for Loewy was:

> How far can the designer go stylewise? This is the all-important question,
> the key to success or failure of a product.
> (Loewy 1951 in Lichtenstein 1990, p.149)

According to the MAYA principle, I can appreciate a design product; it looks good to me. It is elegant, beautiful, and I may want to have it because it is in a way familiar (yet-acceptable), but it has a new design as well (most-advanced). The interpretation and aesthetic appreciation include both familiar and new or unexpected features at the same time. It seems sensible to combine these aspects by Loewy with those discussed by Walton. In the following discussion, I have considered how the signs correspond on one hand to features that are familiar, intentionally designed and related to the product's practical purpose. On the other hand, I determine the features that seem to deviate from them (contra-standard, variable, new, unexpected).

The Domestic Animals project

To illustrate my approach in combining the semantic and the aesthetic, I have chosen the Domestic Animals project by Andrea Branzi (1985–1986) as an example, although its outcome is not an industrial product. By this choice I would like to emphasize the most advanced side of the MAYA principle, which seems aesthetically more challenging than the yet acceptable side. It consists of design products, drawings, an exhibition and a booklet. The products are presented within a frame of a broadly explicated design idea. The idea has been concretized in drawings and design products. The project represents a branch of design that can be called 'experimental design', which does not apply to industrial production requirements. As such it does not include typical design products like the ones analysed in chapter 6. I have chosen this distinct project because it emphasizes innovative aspects and exemplifies this side of design activity. To start with, it seems to state my point more clearly than a commoner product example. The products in Branzi's project are, however, easily recognizable domestic designs like interiors, furniture and things such as vases, carpets and clothes.

I have chosen one of these products for a more detailed study (figure 48).

The sawn parts of a tree trunk and the branches are samples referring to themselves as natural objects with the help of their own properties. They refer also through resemblance to products of forest technology, to half-finished logging and to the woods, from where they came. The iconic sign is strengthened by exemplification. The reference with similarity to natural objects is strengthened by the display of samples (the branches). A plain

Figure 48. A sofa from the Branzi collection Domestic Animals.

161

construction supports the references. The product is made of only a few parts, and thus the uneven broken details of the back rest (the broken branches) stand out.

The sofa affords sitting but, at the same time, it seems to reject a good sitting posture. Instead it seems more like a bench. The leaning backwards is more like the leaning position used outdoors against a tree trunk.

The material chosen, the way of manufacturing, the composition, the graphics and also the exhibiting deviates from the usual way of 'doing design'. High technology (e.g., the accuracy of the seat measurement) has been combined with a raw wooden surface in an unexpected way (most-advanced, but not yet-acceptable). The use and display of high technology express the idea that technical solutions (accurate measurement) are acceptable in a society. The high-tech quality is displayed side by side with unfinished and 'primitive' features in a domestic context. How can the glaring relation of the high-tech and the natural be perceived?

Branzi clarifies his intentions by criticizing the concept 'normality'. He thinks that hybrids grow in our modern society. Old conceptions concerning the normal and abnormal are no longer valid. New normalities and new standards appear. The project Domestic Animals aims at representing this change and tries to break through the rigid frame of normality. In this new situation, Branzi accepts the potentialities of technical development. The role of technology is, however, pushed to the background. A form that refers to natural objects and 'protruding' nature is visually more powerful in the design.

When I look at the sofa-bench by Branzi (figure 48) as a case of the MAYA principle, it seems to me that it is of only little aesthetic value because it looks too odd. The sofa looks abnormal at first. After becoming familiar with it, its references become clear and, if I accept them, it becomes aesthetically valuable as well (yet-acceptable). The secondary or variable features and the contra-standard features of the sofa can be perceived together with its standard features. The latter gives the object its familiar overall form of a sofa. The other requirement, the 'most-advanced' side of the MAYA principle, was already fulfiled. A thing that first was rejected as abnormal is, in closer view, becoming interesting (due to its semantic component) and I begin to like it.

I have now argued for my aesthetic appreciation of Branzi's sofa-bench and illustrated how aesthetics can be related to the semantics of a thing. With this example I have tried to illustrate the relationship between the semantic and the aesthetic in an analysis of a design product and to show how a thing may function as an aesthetic sign. In choosing a piece of furniture like the sofa as an example, I have also widened the sample material of this study. A sofa is in many ways a very different design product than the four other examples in respect to its history, freedom of form and context of use.

The semantic and aesthetic aspects of two other examples

In this chapter, I have surveyed some conceptions of philosophical aesthetics that may contribute to my study. It seemed to me that what can be called aesthetic features are appreciations of some qualities of the thing. It did not seem sensible to limit the aesthetic to a sense impression of an object only. A narrow conception of the aesthetic as a pleasing sense impression can be combined with a broader conception, the interpretation of the product as a sign. A subjective appreciation is then combined with semantic features (i.e., the interpretation of the product as a sign). Aesthetic appreciation is influenced by previous experience, which may give the interpretation of aesthetic appreciation a content that is broader than the thing itself, and the thing is then seen in a context. Although aesthetic appreciation may be explained as, for example, an experience of the colour composition of a thing, appreciation is, in my view, related to the interpretation of its references. Colours are not perceived as disconnected features.

Especially the arguments by Walton seem useful for my study because they include both semantic aspects and specifically aesthetic considerations that are possibly applicable to design products. In addition, aspects that are close to design thinking can be added to his division of features as, for example, the MAYA principle of Loewy. Loewy takes up the question of style and the innovative aspect of design and combines these two with aesthetic appreciation of the design. In this way a new design is compared with already familiar features in the MAYA principle. A comparison with familiar features during the design process does not mean that designers should adhere to the standard features of a category and just redesign within fixed limits.

For example, the aesthetic evaluation of the E 450 exercise cycle requires that it be viewed in a category (Walton 1987, p.61). This requirement seems to be a problem to start with. The cycle has two dominating categories to choose from since it has been designed for two divergent environments. The cycle can be viewed as part of training equipment and as a domestic piece of furniture. Both views were included in the brief for the designer according to my interview with Heikki Kiiski, its designer (19.8.1993). On the basis of my semantic analysis, the outcome of the new design seems better fit for the training centre and should be interpreted in the category of training equipment in the first place. It refers more to training equipment than to domestic furniture. The dynamic composition of the handlebars, saddle and flywheel give the impression of an active form. It expresses motion and affords action. Its many details are familiar from the ordinary bike.

They also remove it further away from home furniture and relate it to sportive items. In a training centre it gives impressions of cleanliness and easy maintenance because of the smooth coverage of the flywheel. Colour seems not to be a decisive factor because a white product can fit in a home as well, depending on the interior and the function of the room, be it a bedroom, a hall, or a bathroom. Colour alternatives would be of help in placing the cycle in a home. The E 450 model expresses solidity and self-assertion. Its style has been designed as part of the company's product line. The graphics have been restricted to the design of the names of the model and the company.

The main variable or secondary feature is the design of the flywheel and its new position in the back. However, the change did not greatly influence its character as a cycle. The references to the type form of a bicycle, its form tradition, seem to be more powerful signs. According to the MAYA principle, the model E 450 looks familiar and is yet acceptable as a cycle and as a piece of training equipment. At the same time it is different (advanced, innovative) when seen in the training centre among other equipment. The visually dynamic design of the flywheel mainly influences this perception. The cycle has a more compact, solid and dynamic overall outlook than other cycles.

Placed in a domestic environment the model E 450 acquires contra-standard features, and it can be conceived as contra-furniture. It lacks standard features of furniture and looks easily like a technical appliance, which may be strange in many home interiors. It would be like bringing a bicycle into the bedroom, which may be an unusual category. In a modern interior or in a teenager's room, which generally includes a broad variation of items in different styles, the cycle would perhaps not seem strange or disconnected. The power of the contra-standard features seems to depend, then, decisively on the character of the interior. Notably, the cycle is not exhibited in different home-like environments, but mainly as a singular object or in connection with other training equipment and a sportive user.

In the case of the telephone kiosk, the choice of a category as a frame of evaluation was evident. The kiosk is perceived as part of the urban environment and relates both to buildings and parks as a piece of street furniture belonging to the field called Public Design. As such, it is viewed together with other equipment in a city, as was done in the semantic analysis.

The telephone m-89 kiosk has standard features, such as the tower-like upright box form, a metal skeleton, transparency and green colour. Because of its plain form it seems almost to have no secondary or contra-standard features. The intention of its designer, according to my interview with him (Juhani Pallasmaa 3.9.1993), was a 'minimalistic' product in which the aesthetically valuable form is achieved by means of composition, proportion and material, which should form a whole. The reduction may be a consequence as in the 'minimal art' tradition (Johnson 1982, p.105–123; Sandqvist 1988, p.303–351). The kiosk does not represent a mere standard product or a dull non-expressive form. The aim is a minimum of associations, a non-illusionistic thing, a cool thing, an autonomous thing, a thing as a thing in itself. In the designer's view art and design are not strictly separable fields, but overlapping. In the aesthetic evaluation of the kiosk I have taken the designer's intentions into account and asked whether the outcome corresponds with the artistic aims. Although I do not conceive the kiosk as an objet d'art, it can surely be understood as partaking in the 'minimal art' tradition on the basis of the semantic analysis. Getting to know the designer's or artist's intentions facilitates my aesthetic appreciation in the case of the kiosk.

The anthropomorphic references of the kiosk, put forward by its critic, turn against the designer's intention and the minimalistic ideas. This criticism shows only that the designer is not in control of the interpretations of his work, and it awakens conflicting ideas. In my view, the intention of the designer should be made explicit in an aesthetic evaluation to promote the discussion of its aesthetic value. It follows then that an aesthetic evaluation of a kiosk is easier to support than the appreciation of the exercise cycle.

Seen within the MAYA principle, the m-89 kiosk seems yet-acceptable according to the semantic analysis. Standard features appear clearly. Its secondary features are related to climatic conditions, when light is reflected on its glassy surfaces or when snow and ice 'decorate' the box in winter time. A contra-standard feature might be its lightness, because the standard form of the kiosk is heavy. The kiosk has been a solid construction in cast iron, wood and steel. Other pieces in its environment contrast to its light character. Is the kiosk innovative enough to provide arguments for aesthetic appreciation? Stretched far in the minimalistic direction and reduced to a plain overall form with the distinct materials on display, it may seem advanced enough. The kiosk attracts attention as a material composition, as a thing in itself.

The kiosk was seen by its critics as too austere and bare when compared with decorated and more solid kiosks of the past. Protection against vandalism was mentioned as the only cause for the plain design by the critics, who then disregarded the aesthetic aims of the designer. They managed to avoid seeing its elegant construction and sensual qualities. Against the background of the commentary in the press, the kiosk can be perceived as most-advanced, since it deviates from more traditional models.

However, design ideals in Finland are often considered to be simplicity, honest display of the material, modest appearance and clear functionality without concealing ornament and extra decoration. At the same time, the kiosk is related to main stream Finnish design conceptions. Other Finnish specialists in design have approved the kiosk, and it has been exhibited among outstanding Finnish designs at the Museum for Applied Arts in Helsinki. The balancing of the aspects of the MAYA principle brings into light different aesthetic appreciations that can be argued for. The main point in evaluating the kiosk is not its familiarity and its standard features (the yet-acceptable side). The most important factor for an evaluation, determined on the basis of the arguments that have already been presented in this discussion, is the overall form, especially its plainness. This quality makes the kiosk even most-advanced in its urban public context.

The preceding discussion, with the help of two products of my examples, illustrates the approach taken to the aesthetic appreciation of design products and its relationship to semantic analysis. Both products were designed by Finnish designers. Their intentions concerning the designs were analysed on the basis of interviews. However, one can argue whether the designer's intention is a significant factor in the evaluation. Does it not suffice to interpret the product with the help of background material, which also includes information about its origin, and then argue for an aesthetic appreciation? Is an emphasis on the designer's intentions a relic of an analysis of a work of art?

In my view, it seems reasonable and even useful to take the designer's intentions into account because a designed product is being examined. The product is not being examined merely because it is used or has a function. Explicated aims and ideas of the design then become important since they enable a person to compare them with the outcome. The explicated intentions concerning the design are seen as a background for the aesthetic evaluation of the design.

7 DISCUSSION

The objective of my investigation was to show how design products can be analysed semantically. The semantics of a product can be approached by asking in what way a product represents its purpose, expresses something or refers to something when it is interpreted. Semiotic research has provided many means for interpreting this type of signification and reference. Therefore I have examined more closely the question of how the semiotic approach suits the study of product semantics. Is a sign necessary, or is the mere recognition that a product, through its visual form, has expressive characteristics enough, as has already been illustrated earlier in the psychology of perception (Arnheim 1974, p.451)?

Signs have proved to be beneficial because, with their help, other types of references can be added to the characteristics of the psychology of perception. According to the semiotic philosophy of Charles S. Peirce the sign of a product refers to something when it is interpreted (*CP* 8.335; *CP* 8.346). In Peirce's semiotics, a product can be considered as a material sign vehicle. The sign is not differentiated from the concrete product. In my opinion, this concept is important in design when concrete products are being planned.

> . . . a sign is something by knowing which we know something more.
> (*CP* 8.332)

The interpretation of a product as a sign adds something to the perception and understanding. Features of form tradition and style, metaphors, indications of use by the form, traces of production, graphic patterns and the like can be interpreted as different references of a product; in other words, they can be analysed as signs. They give an impression of the product and characterize it. Analysing a product as a sign, one can give its representation many kinds of meanings, but the interpretation does not have to be confused, or merely haphazard or silent. A sign can help combine two viewpoints, that of the principles of the psychology of perception and that of the references belonging to interpretation. Therefore, the application of signs in the analysis of design products allows new viewpoints that aid the handling of the representational characteristics of a product. The interpretation of visual (also tactile and auditory) references with the aid of icons, indices and symbols organizes the representation of a product in a new manner that encourages discussion of the reference meanings and a consideration of the route of references. In this manner one could argue for the practicality and suitability of the references in a specific context of use.

Is a sign a simplification and therefore incorrect for the semantic analysis of a product? A theoretical presentation of something, such as the design product in this study, is always misguided if it imagines that it presents all aspects of the object in question and does not see that it attempts to present only certain characteristics for examination (Niiniluoto 1980, p.206). The feasibility of the theory appears in its level of interest and its ability to present the characteristics that are the objectives of research and that can be supported. Peirce's semiotic sign helped the analysis to proceed because it stimulated the differentiation of the references. In addition the sign added versatility to the semantic characteristics that other investigations had considered in a narrower sense.

Interpretation is a part of semantic analysis; in other words, semantic analysis includes a person's concepts of a product. The subjective side of this question was especially considered in connection with iconic signs. I examined the interpretation of the iconic sign as a part of the lifeworld which helps organize a person's perceptions. In phenomenological research the physical product is however parenthesized because the object of study is the structure of consciousness and meaning as intentionalities (Husserl 1970, p.152, 168, and 175). My investigation therefore differs from the phenomenological approach even though the idea of the lifeworld is similar in both (Johansen 1993, p.277).

When an object that has been in use for a long time breaks, its owner can experience more than mere material loss. When parents sell a summer place and all that goes with it, one can say that they have sold more than its material structures. They, at the same time, have sold some of their children's childhood. Children do not necessarily miss the material goods; instead it is the memories of childhood to which the objects (the signs) refer that are a part of their inner being. They miss the lost part of their self that was objectified in the product. The primarily financial, technical or practical attitude of the parents did not take into account the semantic aspect (the significance) of the objects, nor could it understand the loss and possible negative effects of the action.

Survey studies have shown that such semantic characteristics have an important role in the relationship between people and things (Csikszentmihalyi and Rochberg-Halton 1981; Kjellman 1993). The meanings that are people's experiences and conceptions of products cannot however be designed. The references and significances that form a product are different. They are concrete material forms whose references can be intentional even though they are not unchangeable and interpreted all alike.

The subjective iconic sign

The question of the subjective aspect of interpreting a sign is important, especially when an iconic sign is being considered. The limits of semiotic interpretation and also the limits of this analysis become apparent in this process. It can then be said that my analysis represents the viewpoint, which is both European and Finnish, of a designer-trained female researcher in the 1990s. Nor can I start with the attitude that another interpretation might completely accept or even agree with my work even if the work is diverse and well founded. The interpretation that I present is one of the many possible interpretations and does not intend to exclude the others. On the contrary, my interpretation (along with its arguments) functions in a situation in which other possible interpretations participate, and an under-estimation of differing iconic symbols would not be justified. Therefore my interpretation of the products included in this study can be considered a beginning, a part of a discussion, not an end. In the continuing sign production process different interpretations can introduce their own iconic signs.

Signs in cultural contexts

An issue close to this theme of discussion is the way in which language is used to express one's interpretation of a design product. This study aims at furthering the use of conceptual thinking in the discursive practices framed by the context of design.

More is involved than the number and distribution of the sign in the interpretation. The interpretation can help bring attention to the objects of reference (O), the meanings of signs, and the characteristics of the sign vehicles. Peirce's classification of various signs according to the object relation (R–O) is therefore useful.

Context and environment influence the interpretation of signs. The signs of a product cannot be sensibly interpreted if they are considered separately from their context; instead the product must be analysed with the context being taken into account. The situation in which the interpretation takes place affects the sign. According to Johansen (1993, p.291) the frame created for the interpretation by the situation is even a part of the sign. In my opinion, Johansen's point is important because it emphasizes the dependence of the interpretation on context, which creates the setting for the interpretation.

Eco (1979) has treated the settings as semantic fields in which products are analysed as cultural units. For example, one can create a setting in which to examine a bicycle helmet by considering it as a protective device in traffic. Another setting or frame provides other aspects. For example, when it is regarded as a piece of equip-

172

ment used by well-known competitive cyclists or an item targeted for children (MET 1993; Bell 1994), which, in the latter case, has been decorated with letters of the alphabet, infantile ornaments or current motion picture stars such as dinosaurs. The decorations added to the helmet are then signs used in a certain context or semantic field. As signs they can be used to characterize cultural features and values.

Especially interesting in the study of design is the analysis of products by comparing them with earlier models and other models in use. It is not meaningful to analyse products individually or separately because the comparison can reveal conflicting demands on the design and also these conflicting demands can affect the semantic interpretation of a product. A new product such as the bicycle helmet makes a statement in relation to other models when they are compared. Top competitive equipment may be used for the comparison, or it is possible to attempt to adapt the helmet to everyday cycling and bicycles. The design can attempt to please the user when, for instance, the helmet is designed to resemble the one used by Claudio Ciapucci so that the cyclist will have no reason to be ashamed of its use. Or, when a child's helmet is decorated with letters of the alphabet because the parents of first-graders value knowledge of the alphabet. Through design one can affect people's concepts of a product both as buyers, who have expectations with respect to the product, and as users, who are influenced by other people's approval.

Critique of the sign

There is no established procedure for applying a semiotic sign in design studies. A sign is often presented in a complicated manner (Eco 1972). On the other hand, it is often restricted and made banal, whereafter an attempt is made to discard it. When Krippendorff (1984 and 1992) left the analysis of the semiotic sign unfinished, the impression remained that his analysis had been too superficial. Unless the sign is analysed, general conclusions cannot be drawn about its application to

essarily be condemned. The fault is in the neglect of other important characteristics of the design product, and therefore the design product does not fulfil its requirements (as an object of use). Neglect has then weakened the quality of the design product even though the semantics of the product are a success. Similar negative consequences can occur if some other part of a product is neglected. Then the product as a whole becomes distorted; for example, when the material of a product wears out one-sidedly, the user of the product makes mistakes or feels uncomfortable.

Because of their visual training, designers are usually sensitive to the perception of iconic signs. But in technologically and functionally emphasized design metaphoric reference can, for example, be given too little attention. It can depreciatingly be considered strictly a fanciful feature that does not belong among the actual characteristics of practical equipment and can be left outside of design. Even though a metaphor is not knowingly made a part of the design or it is not included in the idea of the form, a product can still be interpreted as a metaphor, and this possibility cannot be sidestepped.

Metaphors can be experienced as telling and unambiguous references. On the other hand, they can seem far-fetched and therefore irrelevant. They are not always very strong and stable references, and they can be indefinite and merely hinting. When the form of a product is described verbally, metaphors sometimes appear, but during the use of a product they can remain in the background.

When designers need to consider signs and take a stand on the representation of a product, they, at the same time, take a stand on the values related to representational qualities. Therefore principles of the psychology of perception do not suffice as arguments for the design. One cannot be satisfied with the description of composition, rhythm, weight, dynamics or harmony, for example, of the psychology of perception. Products should also be interpreted as expressions and representations of a broader cultural context.

The analysis of signs can encourage designers to find new solutions. For an environment that is too simplistic, that can be experienced as banal, designers can plan signs to enrich the environment and signs that are something other than the individual designer's impulses. The designed references can be something other than the culturally abstract composed forms and colours that follow the principles of the psychology of perception.

Knowledge of a product's ecological effects and the ecological circumstances of the earth can be combined with a semantic analysis of the product. Designed references can diversify the perception of an ecological product that cannot have a homogeneous style and a faded colour scheme only. In addition, the semantic analysis of a design product can be combined with consumer studies, which, even today, include design far too seldom. The analysis can add interest in the product environment outside the professional circle of designers, especially among people who work with designers and design products. People are interested in the expression of an object, its effect, and also in the improved control of these characteristics. These features cannot be evaluated exclusively according to subjective likings, even though there can be many different opinions of them.

The analysis of signs can help the attitude taken towards design. The professional language of designers can be developed to be more natural and sensitive. Professional vocabulary can be formed from various signs on the basis of their more general means of reference.

The semiotic sign and various semiotic models have been applied mainly to verbal language and different types of text. When the object of study is a material design product, the difference from language should be distinguishable in the application of the sign. The representational qualities of a design product are closely related to its material and technical qualities. A word does not have similar limits. A product's visual composition also differs from the structure of a sentence. For the product the question is the principles of the psychology of perception not grammar. Therefore, linguistic methods and means of analysing text cannot be directly applied to the study of design products.

The semantic analysis of design can be further developed in a more visual direction, especially when one wants to report the results of the analysis. In place of explicit verbal description the results can be presented by adding depictive material, for example, an exhibition, a video or cartoons, with which the pictures can be made more accurate with text. This type of presentation also requires suitable and consistent concepts. By separating the various modes of sign functioning, I have strived to diversify and illustrate the interpretation of products and help the discussion of their representational qualities. To fulfil this objective, I have explicitly clarified the constitution of the sign in the case of a design product and illustrated its sign character. These are the original results of my study. No earlier studies have so multifariously presented how a design product can function as a sign and how its references can be interpreted as signs from the design point of view. Diverse interpretation is necessary for understanding the nature of a design product when regarded as more than a practical tool.

Design products have not been so concretely analysed as signs with the aid of examples and related background material as in this study. Semantics has generally been a separate addition in which the connection to the design products has remained weak and the possibilities for application have not even been indicated. New in this study is also the grouping of references. The grouping was meant to be an aid for interpretation as I strived to show the variety and coverage of representation, not the finality of my interpretation.

In the literature on design a communication model based on information theory is presented in which the designer is the sender and the user is the receiver. They are depicted as functioning separately and on opposite sides of the signal (product, channel, message) (Bense 1971, p.25; Maser 1976, p.42; Krippendorff 1984, p.5–6; Bürdek 1991, p.135; Quarante 1994, p.319). In the analysis of products as signs this arrangement seemed to lock the positions of interpretation. One can ask how suitable it is for the study of design. The communication model emphasizes the confrontation of the sender and receiver when the designer plans on one hand and someone else receives the plan on the other. The interpreter, that is, the person in the receiver's position, can also be the designer of the object even before the final product is on the market within reach of the user. In addition, in the initial phase of product development the interpretation of signs can be produced by individual designers in a broader working group to which people other than designers belong. Therefore the receiver is not always as distant from the sender as in the model. Feedback about design can be obtained by means other than marketing research or consumer studies. In the literature on design the model from communication theory seems to omit important phases of design when it examines a situation taken from the end of the design process, where the product has already been planned.

In conjunction with perception, sign interpretation is experiencing and reasoning. The interpretation of signs can take place already when the object of design begins to become concrete, is outlined on paper, and receives a shape.

BIBLIOGRAPHY

Aalto, Kristiina: Höyryrautojen vertailu. Kotitalous- ja kuluttaja-asiain tutkimuskeskus, Julkaisuja 4, Helsinki, 1986.

Ahola, Jussi: Teollinen muotoilu. Otakustantamo 441, Espoo, 1980.

Akner Koler, Cheryl: Sculptural Possibilities in Product Design. In: Vihma, S.(ed.): Objects and Images. Publication series of the University of Industrial Arts Helsinki UIAH A12, Helsinki, 1992, 114–117.

Aldersey-Williams, Hugh: New American Design. Rizzoli, New York, 1988.

Andersson, Philip and Tushman, Michael L.: Technological Discontinuities and Dominant Design: A Cyclical Model of Technological Change. *Administrative Science Quarterly* 35, 1990, 604–633.

Anscombe, G.E.M.: The Subjectivity of Sensation. In: *ajatus* 36. Yearbook of the Philosophical Society of Finland, Helsinki, 1976, 3–18.

Archer, L. Bruce: Artist versus Engineer. *Design* 67, Council of Industrial Design, London, 1954, 13–16.

Archer, L. Bruce: Intuition versus Mathematics. *Design* 90, Council of Industrial Design, London, 1956, 12–19.

Archer, L. Bruce: Systematic Method for Designers (*Design Magazine* No. 172, 174, 176, 181, 185, 188; 1963–1964). Council of Industrial Design, London, Revised edition, 1965.

Archer, L. Bruce: Design Awareness and Planned Creativity in Industry. Office of Design, Department of Industry, Trade and Commerce, Ottawa, and the Design Council of Great Britain, London, 1974.

Arnheim, Rudolf: Art and Visual Perception. The New Version. University of California Press, Berkeley, 1974.

Aro, Jari: Jean Baudrillard'n kriittistä semiotiikkaa. *Tiedotus-tutkimus* 3, 1985, 57–65.

Athavankar, Uday A.: The Semantic Profile of Products. In: Vihma, S.(ed.): Semantic Visions in Design. Publications of the University of Industrial Arts Helsinki UIAH A7, Helsinki, 1990, d1–d31.

Atkinson Stephanie & Mockford, Clive: Product Design. Oxford University Press, Oxford, 1991.

Barnes, W: Ein System elektromedizinischer Geräte. *form* 18, Zeitschrift für Gestaltung, Opladen, 1962, 40–45.

Barthes, Roland: Mythologies. 1954–1956. The Noonday Press, New York, 1990 (twenty-third printing).

Barthes, Roland: Semantics of the Object. 1964. In: Barthes, R.: The Semiotic Challenge. Basil Blackwell, Oxford, 1988, 179–190.

Barthes, Roland: Elements of Semiology. Cape Editions, London, 1967.

Baudrillard, Jean: On Seduction. 1979. In: Baudrillard, J.: Selected Writings. Polity Press, Cambridge, 1988, 149–165.

Baudrillard, Jean: Simulacra and Simulation. 1981. In: Baudrillard, J.: Selected Writings, Polity Press, Cambridge, 1988, 166–184.

Baudrillard, Jean: Fatal Strategies. 1983. In: Baudrillard, J.: Selected Writings. Polity press, Cambridge, 1988, 185–206.

Baudrillard, Jean: Ekstaasi ja rivous (L'autre par lui-même. Habilitation). Gaudeamus, Helsinki, 1987.

Baudrillard, Jean: Amerikka (Amérique). Loki-kirjat, Helsinki, 1991.

Beardsley, Monroe C.: Aesthetics, problems in the philosophy of criticism. 1958. Hackett Publishing Company, Inc., Indianapolis and Cambridge, 1988 (Second edition, second printing).

Bennett, Tony: Really Useless 'Knowledge': A Political Critique of Aesthetics. *Literature and History*, Vol.13, London, 1979, 38–57.

Bense, Max: Zeichen und Design. Agis Verlag, Baden-Baden, 1971.

Bernsen, Jens (ed.): KTAS i gadebilledet/Street Signal KTAS. DD casebook 1, Dansk Designråd / Danish Design Council, Copenhagen, 1985.

Beuck, Helga und Jaspersen, Thomas: "Wenige Juroren haben viel zu sagen...". *form* 101, Zeitschrift für Gestaltung, Seeheim, 1983, 6–9.

Black, Misha: Engineering and Industrial Design. 1972. In: Blake, A.(ed.): The Black Papers on Design. Pergamon Press, Oxford, 1983, 177–196.

Blair, Lucian: CMA launches bicycle-helmet campaign, hopes to reduce roadside carnage. *Canadian Medical Association Journal*, Vol.144, No.11, 1991, 1498–1499.

Blueprint: Anarchists in the post office. London, 1991, 46.

Boeckl, Matthias: Design and Law in the Nineteenth Century. Points of Contact and Divergence in the History of Ideas. In: Pirovano, C. et al.(eds.): History of Industrial Design, Volume Two, Electa, Milano, 1990, 96–107.

Bogatyrev, Petr: Costume as a Sign. 1936. In: Matejka, L. and Titunik, I.R.(eds.): Semiotics of Art. The MIT Press, Cambridge, Mass., 1976, 13–19.

Bonsiepe, Gui: Persuasive Communication: Towards a Visual Rhetoric. *uppercase* 5, Whitefriars, London, 1961, 19–34.

Bourdieu, Pierre: Distinction. Routledge & Kegan Paul, London, 1986.

Bourdieu, Pierre: The historical genesis of a pure aesthetics. *Journal of Aesthetics and Art Criticism* 46, 1987, 201–210.

Branzi, Andrea: Domestic Animals. Thames & Hudson, London, 1987.

Buchanan, Richard: Declaration by Design: Rhetoric, Argument, and Demonstration in Design Practice. In: Margolin, V.(ed.): Design Discourse: history, theory, criticism. The University of Chicago Press, Chicago and London, 1989, 91–109.

Buchanan, Richard: Wicked Problems in Design Thinking. *Design Issues*, Vol. VIII, No. 2, The MIT Press, Spring 1992, 5–21.

Burden, Ian et al.: Design & Designing. Longman, London and New York, 1988.

Bush, Donald J.: Body Icons and Product Semantics. In: Vihma, S.(ed.): Semantic Visions in Design. Publications of the University of Industrial Arts Helsinki UIAH A7, Helsinki, 1990, c1–c14.

Bürdek, Bernhard E.: Aufbruchstimmung vor dem EG-Beitritt: Design in Spanien. *form* 112, Zeitschrift für Gestaltung, Seeheim, 1985, 91.

Bürdek, Bernhard E.: Design: Geschichte, Theorie und Praxis der Produktgestaltung. DuMont Buchverlag, Köln, 1991.

Canby, Edward T.: Geschichte der Elektrizität. Editions Rencontre, Lausanne, 1963.

Carlson, Kristina: Kioski keskellä kaupunkia. *Suomen kuvalehti* 34, Helsinki, 1988, 40–44.

Collingwood, R.G.: The Principles of Art. Oxford University Press, 1938.

Conway, Patricia L.: Developing the Product 10: telephone booths. *Industrial Design*, July, 1965, 59–65.

Csikszentmihalyi, Mihaly and Rochberg-Halton, Eugene: The meaning of things. Domestic symbols and the self. Cambridge University Press, Cambridge, 1981.

Design 152: Directions: new products and ideas from abroad. London, 1961, 63.

Design 158: News. London, 1962, 73.

Design 173: Street furniture. London, 1963, 47.

Design 395: Class of '81. London, 1981, 50.

Design 437: BT abandons its thin red line. London, 1985, 15.

Design 473: A high level of mediocrity. London, 1988, 26–29.

Design 482: Putting Safety First. London, 1989, 30–33.

Design 492: Going public. London, 1989, 17.

Design 500: Hive of industry. London, 1990, 16.

Design 502: Telephone booths. London, 1990, 68.

Design 518: Brits try out the Triennale. London, 1992, 53.

Design Forum 2: Pro Finnish Design palkintoehdokkaat. Suomalaisen muotoilun edistämiskeskuksen lehti, Helsinki, 1992, 3–7.

DiGuiseppi, Carolyn G. et al.: Bicycle Helmet Use by Children. Evaluation of a Community-wide Helmet Campaign. *The Journal of the American Medical Association* (JAMA), Vol.262, No.16, 1989, 2256–2261.

Dorfles, Gillo: Gute Industrieform und ihre Ästhetik. Verlag Moderne Industrie, München, 1964

Dorfles, Gillo: The Man-Made Object. In: Kepes, G.(ed.): the man-made object. Studio Vista, London, 1966, 1–8.

Eco, Umberto: Function and Sign: The Semiotics of Architecture. 1968. In: Broadbent, G. et al.(eds.): Signs, Symbols, and Architecture. John Wiley & Sons, Chichester, 1980, 11–70

Eco, Umberto: A Theory of Semiotics. Indiana University Press, Bloomington, 1979.

Eco, Umberto: A Componental Analysis of the Architectural Sign /Column/. 1972. In: Broadbent, G. et al.(eds.): Signs, Symbols, and Architecture. John Wiley & Sons, Chichester, 1980, 213–232.

Ehrnrooth, Lotta: Höyrysilitysrauta sopii kiireiselle silittäjälle. *Kuluttaja* 4, Helsinki, 1994, 38–42.

Escherle, Hans-Jürgen: Industrie-Design für ausländische Märkte. (Diss.) GBI-Verlag, München, 1986.

Eskola, Antti: Sosiologian tutkimusmenetelmät 1. WSOY, Helsinki, 1981 (Neljännen painoksen toinen muuttamaton lisäpainos).

Farm, Cristina: Tuffa killar trampar trendhoj. *Råd & rön* 6–7, Stockholm, 1992, 12–14.

Farm, Cristina: Grönt spänne för små cyklister. *Råd & rön* 4, Stockholm, 1994, 20.

Findeli, Alain: Design Education and Industry: the Laborious Beginnings of the Institute of Design in Chicago in 1944. *Journal of Design History*, Vol.4, No.2, 1991, 97–113.

form 72: Blickpunkte von der Kongress-Umwelt. Zeitschrift für Gestaltung, Seeheim, 1975, 9.

form 85: Ein Design – Wettbewerb der Bundespost – gesucht: eine Telefonzelle für Rollstuhlfahrer. Zeitschrift für Gestaltung, Seeheim, 1979, 12–17.

form 92: Design-Umfeld. Zeitschrift für Gestaltung, Seeheim, 1980, 56.

form 115: Die Post suchte ein neues Häuschen. 5 Entwurfsvorschläge, die der Post gefallen. Zeitschrift für Gestaltung, Seeheim-Jugendheim, 1986, 52–53.

form 133: Ludwigsburger Design für die Schweiz. Zeitschrift für Gestaltung, Seeheim, 1991, 70.

Form 1955: Gatans detaljer. Svenska Slöjdföreningens förlag, Stockholm, 1955.

Form 8: Advertisement by Monark. Svenska Slöjdföreningens tidskrift, Stockholm, 1967, 491.

Form 9: Formrevy. Svenska Slöjdföreningens tidskrift, Stockholm, 1968, 586.

Form 1971: Gatans möbler. Stockholm, 1971, 78–79.

Form 7: Gothenburg School of Industrial Art. Stockholm, 1986, 40.

Friedländer, Uri: An Historical Perspective on the New Wave in Design. *innovation*, The Journal of the Industrial Designers Society of America, Spring 1984, 12–15.

Føllesdal, Dagfinn: The Lebenswelt in Husserl. In: Haaparanta, L. et al.(eds.): Language, Knowledge, and Intentionality. Acta Philosophica Fennica, Vol.49, Helsinki, 1990, 123–143.

Garner, Steve: Human Factors. Oxford University Press, Oxford, 1991.

Garnich, Rolf: Konstruktion Design Ästhetik. (Diss.) Selbstverlag, Stuttgart, 1968.

Gibson, James J.: On Theories for Visual Space Perception. 1970. In: Reed, E. and Jones, R.(eds.): Reasons for Realism. Lawrence Erlbaum Associates, Hillsdale, New Jersey, 1982, 76–89.

Gibson, James J.: The Myth of Passive Perception: A Reply to Richards. 1976. In: Reed, E. and Jones, R.(eds.): Reasons for Realism. Lawrence Erlbaum Associates, Hillsdale, New Jersey, 1982, 397–400.

Gibson, James J.: The Theory of Affordances and the Design of the Environment. 1976. In: Reed, E. and Jones, R.(eds.): Reasons for Realism. Lawrence Erlbaum Associates, Hillsdale, New Jersey, 1982, 413–416.

Giedion, Sigfried: Mechanization Takes Command. 1948. Oxford University Press, New York, 1955 (Second Printing).

Goldman, Alan H.: Aesthetic Qualities and Aesthetic Value. *The Journal of Philosophy*, Vol.LXXXVII, 1990, 23–37.

Gombrich, Ernst: Art and Illusion, Phaidon Press, London, 1968 (Third Edition).

Goodman, Nelson: Languages of Art. 1976. Hacket Publ.Co., Indianapolis, 1985 (Fifth Printing).

Gray, John: GPO miscellany. *Design* 122, London, 1959, 65.

Greimas, Algirdas J. and Courtés Joseph: Semiotics and Language. Indiana University Press, Bloomington, 1982.

Gros, Jochen: Grundlagen einer Theorie der Produktsprache. Einführung. Heft 1, Hochschule für Gestaltung Offenbach am Main, 1983.

Gros, Jochen: Das zunehmende Bedürfnis nach Form. *form* 107, Zeitschrift für Gestaltung, Seeheim, 1984a, 11–15.

Gros, Jochen: Reporting Progress Through Product Language. *innovation*, The Journal of the Industrial Designers Society of America, Spring 1984b, 10–11.

Gros, Jochen: Grundlagen einer Theorie der Produktsprache. Symbolfunktionen. Heft 4, Hochschule für Gestaltung Offenbach am Main, 1987.

Groupe μ: Iconism. In: Sebeok, T.A. and Sebeok, J.(eds.): Advances in Visual Semiotics. Mouton de Gruyter, Berlin and New York, 1995, 21–46.

Gugelot, Hans: design als zeichen. 1962. In: Wichmann, H.(Hrsg.): System-Design Bahnbrecher: Hans Gugelot 1920–1965. Die Neue Sammlung, München, 1984, 43–50.

Haapala, Arto: Maku- ja taidearvostelmat. *Synteesi* 3, Helsinki, 1991, 64–76.

Hahn, Peter und Engelbrecht, Lloyd, C.(Hrsg.): 50 Jahre New Bauhaus. Bauhausnachfolge in Chicago. Bauhaus-Archiv, Argon Verlag GmbH, Berlin, 1987.

Hanley, John: Bicycle Safety – What's new in '92? *Journal of the Florida Medical Association*, Vol.78, No.5, 1991, 229–230.

Hardyment, Christina: From Mangle to Microwave. The Mechanization of Household Work. Polity Press and Basil Blackwell, Oxford, 1988.

Heidegger, Martin: Der Ursprung des Kunstwerkes. In: Heidegger, M.: Holzwege. Gesamtausgabe, Band 5, Vittorio Klostermann, Frankfurt am Main, 1977, 1–74.

Heiskala, Risto: Tulkinnan koeteltavuus ja aikakauslehtien analyysi. In: Mäkelä, K.(ed.): Kvalitatiivisen aineiston analyysi ja tulkinta. Gaudeamus, Helsinki, 1990, 242–263.

Helsinki Energy: Pyykin jälkikäsittelylaitteet. Helsingin kaupungin energia-laitos, monisteet, 1.12.1988, 1.2.1993, 1.3.1994

Herler, Igor: Yritys hyvä kymmenen, arvosana välttävä kuusi. *Muoto* 4, Teolli-suustaiteen Liitto Ornamo, Helsinki, 1989, 37.

Heufler, Gerhard: Produkt-Design...von der Idee zur Serienreife. Veritas-Verlag, Linz, 1987.

Hintikka, Jaakko: Kieli ja mieli. Otava, Helsinki, 1982.

Hjelte, Gudrun: EG sponsrar hjälmkonferens. *Råd & rön* 3, Stockholm, 1993, 26–27.

Hufnagl, Florian: Street Furniture. In: Typical Objects from the Industrial Design Department. Die Neue Sammlung, State Museum for Applied Art and Design, München, 1981.

Hufnagl, Florian (ed.): Design und Kunst: Burg Giebichenstein 1845–1990. Die Neue Sammlung, Staatliches Museum für angewandte Kunst, München, 1991,43.

Husserl, Edmund: Husserliana Band III. Martinus Nijhoff, Den Haag, 1950, 59.

Husserl, Edmund: Husserliana Band IV. Martinus Nijhoff, Haag, 1952, 375.

Husserl, Edmund: The Crisis of European Sciences and Transcendental Phenomenology. Northwestern University Press, Evanston, 1970.

Hämäläinen, Vesa et al.: Polkupyöräilijä liikenteessä. Liikenneturva, Helsinki, 1992.

ICSID: The Education of Industrial Designers. Report of a Seminar 21–24.3.1964, Bruges, 1965.

Industrial Design 1960: Advertisement. September, 1960, 48.

Industrial Design 1962: Alcoa Awards. July, 1962, 42.

Industrial Design 1984: Culture and design. March/April, 1984, 55.

Industrial Design 1984: Americas leading design recognition program. July/August, 1984, 63.

Itten, Johannes: Gestaltungs- und Formenlehre. Otto Maier Verlag, Ravensburg, 1973 und 1975.

Jeudy, Henri Pierre: Beyond a Semiology of Objects. In: de Noblet, J.(ed.): Industrial Design, Reflections of a Century. Flammarion, Paris, 1993, 355–360.

Johansen, Jørgen Dines: Let sleeping signs lie: On signs, objects, and communication. *Semiotica* 97, Walter de Gruyter, 1993, 271–295.

Johnson, Ellen H. (ed.): American Artists on Art from 1940 to 1980. Harper & Row, Publishers, New York, 1982.

Junttila, Ulla-Kirsti: Muotoilu julkisessa ympäristössä. Unpublished diploma work, University of Art and Design Helsinki UIAH, 1978.

Junttila, Ulla-Kirsti: Muuttuvat kadun kalusteet, Rakennuskirja Oy, Helsinki, 1986.

Kanerva, Thea: Monitoimikoneiden vertailu. Kotitalous- ja kuluttaja-asiain tutki-muskeskus, Julkaisuja 7, 1988.

Kellner, Petra und Poessnecker, Holger: Produktgestaltung an der HfG Ulm. Designtheorie Band 3, Hanau, 1978.

Kempas Martti ja Pajunen Raimo (toim.): Pyöräily – kuntoa, vauhtia, virkistystä. Valmennuskolmio Oy, Jyväskylä, 1987.

Kepes, Gyorgy: language of vision. Paul Theobald and Company, Chicago, 1959.

Kepes, Gyorgy (ed.): Sign, Image and Symbol. Studio Vista, London, 1966.

Kicherer, Sibylle: Industriedesign als Leistungsbereich von Unternehmen. (Diss.) GBI-Verlag, München, 1987.

Kinross, Robin: Semiotics and designing. *Information design journal*, Vol.4/3, Milton Keynes, 1986, 190–198.

Klöcker, Ingo: Die Produkt-Form und menschliches Verhalten. Eine Unter-suchung von psycho-physiologischen Ursachen und Wirkungen, Elementen und Kriterien der Gestaltung von Geräten, Maschinen, Anlagen und Fahrzeugen. (Diss.) Technische Universität Hannover, 1980.

Koivurova, Matti: Pyöräilyvammat ja -kypärät. Liikenneturva, Helsinki, 1993.

Krampen, Martin: Survey of Current Work on the Semiology of Objects. In: Chatman, S. et al.(eds.): A Semiotic Landscape. Mouton Publishers, The Hague, 1979, 158–168.

Krampen, Martin: Design. In: Sebeok, T.A.(ed.): Encyclopedic Dictionary of Semiotics, Mouton de Gruyter, Berlin, 1986, 187–190.

Krampen, Martin: Objects. In: Sebeok, T.A.(ed.): Encyclopedic Dictionary of Semiotics. Mouton de Gruyter, Berlin, 1986, 635–639.

Krampen, Martin: Semiotics in Architecture and Industrial/Product Design. *Design Issues*, Volume V, No.2, The MIT Press, 1989, 124–140.

Krippendorff, Klaus and Butter, Reinhart: Product Semantics: Exploring the Symbolic Qualities of Form. *innovation*, The Journal of the Industrial Designers Society of America, Spring 1984, 4–9.

Krippendorff, Klaus: Die Produktsemantik öffnet die Türen zu einem neuen Bewusstsein im Design. *form* 108/109, Zeitschrift für Gestaltung, Seeheim, 1985, 14–16.

Krippendorff, Klaus: On the Essential Contexts of Artifacts or On the Proposition That "Design is Making Sense (of Things)". *Design Issues*, Vol.V, No.2, The MIT Press, 1989, 9–39.

Krippendorff, Klaus: Transcending Semiotics: Towards Understanding Design for Understanding. In: Vihma, S.(ed.): Objects and Images. Publication series of the University of Industrial Arts Helsinki UIAH A12, Helsinki, 1992, 24–47.

Kristofferson Sandström, Ylva: Strykning kräver tålamod och mycket ånga. *Råd & rön* 5, Stockholm, 1992, 27–29.

Krohn, Lisa and McCoy, Michael: Beyond Beige: Interpretive Design for the Postindustrial Age. *Design Issues*, Vol.V, No.2, The MIT Press, 1989, 112–123.

Laine, Vieno: Silitysrautojen vertailu. Kotitalous- ja kuluttaja-asiain tutkimus-keskuksen julkaisuja 4, Helsinki, 1983.

Lammenranta, Markus: Kauneuden välinearvo – Beardsley ja Goodman. Sis: Lammenranta, M. ja Rantala, V.(toim.): Kauneus. Suomen Filosofinen Yhdistys, Tampere, 1990, 189–199.

Lannoch, Helga und Lannoch, Hans-Jürgen: Die Form folgt nicht mehr der elektronischen Funktion. *form* 104, Zeitschrift für Gestaltung, Seeheim, 1983, 28.

Lannoch, Hans-Jürgen: How to Move from Geometric to Semantic Space. *innovation*, The Journal of the Industrial Designers Society of America, Spring 1984, 20–22.

Lannoch, Helga und Lannoch, Hans-Jürgen: Vom geometrischen zum semantischen Raum. *form* 118, Zeitschrift für Gestaltung, Seeheim, 1987, 12–17.

Lannoch, Helga and Lannoch, Hans-Jürgen: Toward a Semantic Notion of Space. *Design Issues*, VOL.V, No.2, The MIT Press, 1989, 40–50.

Larroche, Helene et Tucny, Jan: L'objet industriel. Centre George Pompidou/ CCI, Paris, 1980.

Lehtonen, Aimo: Koululaisen liikenneturvallinen polkupyörä. *Liikennevilkku* 2, 1986, 16–18.

Lichtenstein, Claude: Apostle of Simplicity. Loewy's book Never leave Well Enough Alone. In: Schönberger, A.(ed.): Raymond Loewy. Pioneer of American Industrial Design. Prestel Verlag, München, 1990, 143–149.

Lindinger, Herbert: The Criteria for Good Industrial Design. In: Die gute Industrieform, Hannover, 1982, 8–9.

Lindinger, Herbert: The criteria for good industrial design. In: Prädikat Die gute Industrieform, Hannover, 1983, 9.

Lindinger, Herbert (Hrsg.): ulm...Die Moral der Gegenstände. Wilhelm Ernst & Sohn, Berlin, 1987.

Lindinger, Herbert: The criteria for good industrial design. In: if 89, Industrieform Hannover, 1989, 576.

Lotman, Yuri M.: Universe of the Mind. A Semiotic Theory of Culture. I.B.Tauris & Co. Ltd., London, 1990

Lundgren, Carina: Enkel och robust barncykel...och hjälm ska det va'. *Råd & rön* 3, Stockholm, 1983, 16–18.

Lupton, Ellen: Mechanical Brides: Women and Machines from Home to Office. Cooper-Hewitt National Museum of Design Smithsonian Institution and Princeton Architectural Press, New York, 1993.

Lyytikkä, Terttu et al.: Silitys. Kotitalouskeskuksen tiedotuksia No.14, Helsinki, 1963.

Maldonado, Tomás: Notes on Communication. Non-semantic and semantic orientation. *uppercase* 5, Whitefriars, London, 1961, 5–10.

Maldonado, Tomás: Glossary of Semiotics. *uppercase* 5, Whitefriars, London, 1961, 44–62.

Manzini, Ezio: The Material of Invention. Arcadia Edizioni, Milano, 1986.

Manzini, Ezio: The End of the Mechanical Age. In: Pirovano, C. et al.(eds.): History of Industrial Design. Vol.3, Electa, Milano, 1991, 34–55.

Margolis, Joseph: Art and Philosophy. The Harvester Press, Brighton, 1980.

Maser, Siegfried: Einführung in die Gestaltungstheorie. Unpublished manuscript, Universität-Gesamthochschule Wuppertal, 1981.

Maser, Siegfried: Design as Science. In: Vihma, S.(ed.): Form and Vision. Publication series of the University of Industrial Arts Helsinki UIAH B7, Helsinki, 1987, 90–99.

Mayall, W.H.: Principles in Design. Design Council, London, 1979.

McDermott, Francis T.: Helmets for bicyclists – another first for Victoria. *The Medical Journal of Australia*, Vol.154, 1991, 156–157.

Meisner, Anne och Röhl, Ia: Alla tål inte hårt vatten. *Råd & rön* 6–7, Stockholm, 1994, 25–27.

Metsä–Ketelä, Heikki: Ulmin Hochschule für Gestaltung: ideologiasta ja toiminnasta. In: Melgin, E.(toim.): Ajatus ja sahaus. Taideteollisen korkeakoulun julkaisusarja B4, Helsinki, 1991, 85–94.

Mikkola, Kirmo: Funktionalismin ideologia. *arkkitehti*, ark 1, Helsinki, 1978, 46–52.

Mikkola, Kirmo et al.(toim.): funkis. Suomi nykyaikaa etsimässä. Näyttelyluettelo, Helsinki, 1980 (2 korjattu painos).

Moles, Abraham: Information Theory and Aesthetic Perception. University of Illinois Press, Urbana, 1966.

Morris, Charles: Writings on the General Theory of Signs. Mouton & Co., The Hague, 1971.

Mosso, Leonardo: L'opera di Alvar Aalto. Edizioni di Communità, Milano, 1965.

Mäkelä, Klaus (toim.): Kvalitatiivisen aineiston analyysi ja tulkinta. Gaudeamus, Helsinki, 1990.

Neisser, Ulric (ed.): Concepts and Conceptual development: Ecological and intellectual factors in categorization. Cambridge University Press, Cambridge, 1987.

Niiniluoto, Ilkka: Johdatus tieteenfilosofiaan. Otava, Helsinki, 1980.

Niiniluoto, Ilkka: Tieteellinen päättely ja selittäminen. Otava, Helsinki, 1983.

Niiniluoto, Ilkka: Philosophical Perspectives on Design. In: Vihma, S.(ed.): Designforschung Design Research Symposium. Publication Series of the University of Industrial Arts Helsinki UIAH A1, Helsinki, 1984, 13–31.

Niiniluoto, Ilkka: Tieteenfilosofisia näkökulmia kulttuurintutkimukseen, Ethnosjulkaisu 1, eripainos, Helsinki, 1985.

Niiniluoto, Ilkka: Pragmatismi. In: Niiniluoto, I. ja Saarinen, E.(toim.): Vuosisatamme filosofia. WSOY, Helsinki, 1986, 40–73.

Niiniluoto, Ilkka: Informaatio, tieto ja yhteiskunta. Valtion painatuskeskus, Helsinki, 1989.

Niiniluoto, Ilkka: Kauneus ja informaatio. Sis: Lammenranta, M. ja Rantala, V.(toim.): Kauneus. Filosofisia tutkimuksia Tampereen yliopistosta, Vol.IV, Tampere, 1990, 200–222.

de Noblet, Jocelyn (ed.): Industrial Design, Reflection of a Century. Flammarion, Paris, 1993.

Nordlund, Kai ja Sitari, Esa: Tutkittua tietoa lasten polkupyöristä. *Kuluttajatietoa* 5, Helsinki, 1989, 10–12.

Nummenmaa, Tapio et al.: Yleinen psykologia kokeellisen tutkimuksen valossa. Otava, Helsinki, 1982.

Oehlke, Horst: Produkterscheinung / Produktbild / Produktleitbild. (Diss.) Humboldt-Universität zu Berlin, 1982.

Oehlke, Horst: Zur Zeichentheoretischen Beschreibung von Designobjekten. In: Gestalt und Ausdruck. Funktionales Design und Semiotik. 11. designwissenschaftliches Kolloquium an der Hochschule für industrielle Formgestaltung Halle 25–56.11.1987, Halle, 1988, 141–168.

Olkkonen, Seppo ja Koivurova, Matti: Pyöräilyonnettomuuksia vähennetään teknisillä keinoilla ja asennemuutoksilla. *Suomen Lääkärilehti* 14, Helsinki, 1990, 1331–1336.

Palsanen, Eila: Kodin työvälineoppi. Toinen nide, III Kotitalouskoneet ja kojeet, Otava, Helsinki, 1958.

Patton, Phil: Hard Hats. *I.D.Magazine*, Vol.4, No.3, 1994, 62–66.

Paulsson, Gregor och Paulsson, Nils: Tingens bruk och prägel. Kooperativa förbundets bokförlag, Stockholm, 1956.

Peirce, Charles S.: Collected Papers of Charles Sanders Peirce. vols. 1–8. (Hartshorne, C, Weiss, P, and Burks, A.W. eds.) Harvard University Press, Cambridge, MA, 1931–1966. (References are to volumes and paragraphs, not to pages)

Peirce, Charles S.: The Scientific Attitude and Fallibilism. 1896. In: Peirce, C.S.: The Philosophy of Peirce. Selected Writings. (Buchler, J. ed.) Harcourt, Brace and Company, New York, 1940, 42–54.

Peirce, Charles S.: Critical Common-sensism. 1905. In: Peirce, C.S.: The Philosophy of Peirce. Selected Writings. (Buchler, J. ed.) Harcourt, Brace and Company, New York, 1940, 290–305.

Poisson, Célyne: De l'objet au sujet; pour une sémiotique du projet en design. Unpublished manuscript. Fifth Congress of the International Association for Semiotic Studies, University of California, Berkeley, 1994.

Puomila, Maija: Kypäriä testattiin. *Kuluttaja* 3, Helsinki, 1993, 9.

Quarante, Danielle: Éléments de design industriel. Polytechnica, Paris, 1994 (2e édition).

Radice, Barbara: Memphis. Electa, Milano, 1984.

Rams, Dieter und Ullman, Roland: "Gute Form ist nie vollendet". *form* 108/109, Zeitschrift für Gestaltung, Seeheim, 1984/85, 38–41.

Ray, Man: Photographien Paris 1920–1934. Schirmer/Mosel, München, 1980.

Reese, Jens: Design ist Vohrahnung – nicht Nachahnung. *form* 112, Zeitschrift für Gestaltung, Seeheim, 1985, 20–23.

Rosch, Eleanor: Cognitive Representations of Semantic Categories. *Journal of Experimental Psychology*: General, Vol.104, No.3, 1975, 192–233.

Ross, Kristin: Starting Afresh: Hygiene and Modernization in Postwar France. *October* 67, The MIT Press, Cambridge, 1994, 23–57.

Runyan, Carol W. and Runyan, Desmond K.: How Can Physicians Get Kids to Wear Bicycle Helmets? *American Journal of Public Health*, Vol.81, No.8, 1991, 972–973.

Salovaara, Juhani: Suomi-estetiikan jäljillä. *Muoto* 4, Teollisuustaiteen Liitto Ornamo, Helsinki, 1988, 20–23.

Samson, Jeff: The Cornerstone of Competition. *Design* 473, The Design Council, London, 1988, 21.

Sandqvist, Tom: Den meningslösa kuben. Den minimalistiska bildkonstens teoretiska förutsättningar och bakgrund. Kalejdoskop förlag, Åhus, 1988.

Schürer, Arnold: Der Einfluss Produktbestimmender Faktoren auf die Gestaltung. 1969. (Diss.) Selbstverlag, Bielefeld, 1974. (3. verbesserte Auflage)

Sebeok, Thomas A. et al.(eds.): Encyclopedic Dictionary of Semiotics. Mouton de Gruyter, Berlin, 1986.

Sebeok, Thomas A.: A sign is just a sign. Indiana University Press, Bloomington, 1991.

Selle, Gert: Die Geschichte des Design in Deutschland von 1870 bis heute. Entwicklung der industriellen Produktkultur. DuMont Buchverlag, Köln, 1978 (2. Auflage).

Seppälä, Matti ja Juvela, Seppo: Aivovammojen syyt pääkaupunkiseudulla. *Suomen Lääkärilehti* 21, Helsinki, 1991, 1987–1991.

Sibley, Frank: Aesthetic Concepts. *The Philosophical Review LXVII*, 1959, 421–450.

Silverman, Kaja: The Subject of Semiotics. Oxford University Press, New York, 1983.

Skott, Staffan: Pyöräilijän kirja. Otava, Helsinki, 1986.

Sless, David: Reading semiotics. *Information design journal*, Vol.4/3, Milton Keynes, 1986, 179–189.

Smets, Gerda: Form Semantics: a scientific approach. In: Vihma, S.(ed.): Form and Vision. Publication series of the University of Industrial Arts Helsinki UIAH B7, Helsinki, 1987, 100–113.

Sonesson, Göran: Pictorial Concepts. Lund University Press, Lund, 1989.

Sotamaa, Yrjö: Kurjen huuto ja sininen Saimaa. *Muoto* 3, Teollisuustaiteen Liitto Ornamo, Helsinki, 1987, 66–69.

Sparke, Penny: Design in Context. Bloomsbury, London, 1987a.

Sparke, Penny: Electrical Appliances. Unwyn Hyman, London, 1987b.

Sparke, Penny: Japanese Design. Swallow Publishing Ltd., London, 1987c.

Stamp, Gavin: Telephone Boxes. Chatto & Windus, London, 1989.

Steadman, Philip: The Evolution of Designs. Cambridge University Press, Cambridge, 1979.

Strandh, Sigvard: Maskinen genom tiderna. AB Nordbok, Göteborg, 1979.

Talouselämä 36: Salonkikelpoinen kuntomittari. Helsinki, 1992, 43.

Tatarkiewicz, Wladyslaw: A History of Six Ideas. Polish Scientific Publishers, Warszawa, 1980.

Thompson, Robert S. et al.: A Case-Control Study of the Effectiveness of Bicycle Safety Helmets. *The New England Journal of Medicine*, Vol.320, No.21, 1989, 1361–1367.

Thompson, Diane C. et al.: Incidence of Bicycle Injuries in a Defined Population. *American Journal of Public Health*, Vol.80, No.11, 1990, 1388–1390.

Thompson, Diane C. et al.: A Case-Control Study of the Effectiveness of Bicycle Safety Helmets in Preventing Facial Injury. *American Journal of Public Health*, Vol.80, No.12, 1990, 1471–1474.

Tirkkonen, Marja-Liisa: Every Success has its Story. *Business Finland* 1994, Sanomaprint, Helsinki, 1993, 83–87.

Turpeinen, Oiva: Helsingin seudun puhelinlaitos 1882–1982. Helsingin puhelin-yhdistys, Turun Sanomat, Turku, 1981.

Tylor, E.B.: Primitive Culture I, John Murray, London, 1920.

Walton, Kendall L.: Categories of Art. *The Philosophical Review*, Vol. LXXIX, No.3, 1970, 334–367.

Weidemann, Kurt: Modelle für ein visuelles Erscheinungsbild. *form* 82, Zeitschrift für Gestaltung, Seeheim, 1978, 19–24.

Vihma, Susann: Tuotteen muodon kuvaaminen. (Lic.thesis) Unpublished manuscript, Helsinki, 1990.

Winnicott, Donald W.: Playing and Reality. 1971. Penguin Books Ltd. (Reissued in Pelican Books), Harmondsworth, 1985.

Wingler, Hans M.: The Bauhaus. The MIT Press, Cambridge, MA, 1980.

Wolf, Brigitte: Design für den Alltag. (Diss.) Profil-Verlag, München, 1983.

Väkevä, Seppo: Tuotesemantiikka. Taideteollisen korkeakoulun julkaisusarja A6, Helsinki, 1987.

Zitzmann, Lothar: Grundlagen visueller Gestaltung 1–3. Hochschule für Gestaltung, Halle, 1984, 1985 und 1987.

The following persons have been interviewed for collecting background material of sample material:

Jasmine **Julin**,	fashion designer
Jyrki **Järvinen**,	industrial designer
Ilkka **Kettunen**,	industrial designer
Heikki **Kiiski**,	industrial designer
Mariaana **von Knorring**,	ass. professor of fashion design
Karl–Erik **Nordström**,	coordinator
Juhani **Pallasmaa**,	professor of architecture
Matti **Seppänen**,	fashion designer
Teppo **Vienamo**,	industrial designer

Brochures and advertisements

1. Brochures about steam irons:

AEG, Pienlaitteet, Sähköliikkeiden OY, Vantaa.
Bernina, 1993
Braun kotitalouskoneet, Helsinki, 1985.
Braun tuotekuvasto 1994/95
Elram, 1994
Jura, 1993
Kenwood, 1994
Krups, 1993
Mia, 1994
Moulinex, Euroopan suurin pienlaitevalmistaja. 1988.
Moulinex, 1993
Philips, Kutsuva keittiö. Kalusteisiin sijoitetut Philips–kodinkoneet, Helsinki, 1988.
Philips, Pienet kodinkoneet, 1992
Philips, Siistiä ja sileää, Espoo, 1994
Philips, Kodinkoneet tuoteluettelo '95
Rowenta, Kodin pienkoneet, edistyksellistä tekniikkaa ja muotoilua. 1989.
Rowenta, 1994
Severin, Kodin pienkoneita, 1993 ja 1994
Tefal, 1988 and 1994

2. Brochures and advertisement about exercise cycles:

Air machine home fitness 1991
Karhu Oy, fitness equipment 1991
Kerko sport, kuntosalilaitteet 1992
Kettler Sport, Kuntovälineet
Monark, (advertising pictures in Form 1967, p.491 and 1968, p.599)
Stockmann, Kanta–asiakkaan edut, October 1993
Tunturi, Kuntoväline–esitteet 1990, 1992, 1993 ja 1994
Wrange, kuntokuvasto 1/1993

Kotilääkäri 11/1988, s.14–15
Kuntoplus 4/1989 s.16–18
Talouselämä 36, 1992, s.43.

3. Brochures about bicycle helmets:

Bell Sports Inc., models (USA) 1993
Bell Sports Inc., models (USA) 1994
Diamond Back bicycles 1994
Helkama, Lasten/nuortenpyörät 1993
Helkama, Maastoretkipyörät 1993
Helkama, MTB/ATB
Helkama–pyörä, kypäräesite
MET, Pyöräilijän kypärien esite
Polar Elektro Oy
Tunturi, polkupyöräesite 1993
Profile (USA)
Liikenneturva, Parempi katsoa kuin katua, esite 1991
Liikenneturva ja Liikenneministeriö, esite 1994
Trafikskyddet, brochure (Sweden)

Photographs on the colour pages:

page 1. by Susann Vihma
page 2. by Liikemainonta–McCann Oy
page 3. by Soile Tirilä
page 4. by Soile Tirilä

NAME INDEX

Anscombe, G.E.M. 79, 80, 85

Archer, L. Bruce 11, 104

Arnheim, Rudolf 115, 45–46, 169

Barthes, Roland 10, 25, 72, 87, 88, 176

Baudrillard, Jean 73, 174,

Beardsley, Monroe C. 153

Bense, Max 23–24, 27, 61

Bogatyrev, Petr 10, 21

Bonsiepe, Gui 23

Bourdieu, Pierre 88, 156

Branzi, Andrea 161–162

Butter, Reinhart 41

Csikszentmihalyi, Mihaly and Rochberg-Halton, Eugene 27–29, 82,154,171,176

Dorfles, Gillo 11,13, 22, 59

Eco, Umberto 10, 13, 59, 62, 64, 77, 85, 146, 154, 172

Gibson, James J. 45–49

Gombrich, Ernst 89, 156

Goodman, Nelson 42, 69, 77, 151, 152, 153, 156

Gros, Jochen 11, 38–40

Gugelot, Hans 11, 13, 15, 21, 22

Haapala, Arto 154, 156

Heidegger, Martin 48, 51

Husserl, Edmund 81, 83, 170

Kepes, Gyorgy 49

Kicherer, Sibylle 15–16, 21, 43

Klöcker, Ingo 11, 14, 17, 34–37, 43, 52, 57, 95, 118

Krippendorff, Klaus 11, 22, 41–43, 63, 173

Lannoch, Helga and Lannoch, Hans-Jürgen 17, 40–41, 48, 52

Lindinger, Herbert 20

Loewy, Raymond 14, 160

Maldonado, Tomás 11, 22, 31

Maser, Siegfried 27

Morris, Charles 22

Niiniluoto, Ilkka 18, 22, 45–47, 50, 56, 78, 170

Oehlke, Horst 11, 43, 59

13

LIST OF APPENDICES

1   Iconic, indexical, and symbolic groups of references of a design product

2   Previous analyses of design products

3   The steam irons chosen as examples for the study, the steam irons in a user analysis (Aalto 1986) and steam iron models on the market in Helsinki in 1989 and 1994. Pictures of the models of the sample material. Technical and ergonomic aspects considered and measured for the semantic analysis

4   Technical and ergonomic aspects of the E 450 cycle

5   Technical and ergonomic aspects of the m-89 kiosk

6   Technical and ergonomic aspects of the MET Skymaster helmet

A1 ICONIC, INDEXICAL, AND SYMBOLIC GROUPS OF REFERENCES OF DESIGN PRODUCTS

Iconic sign references

1. The tradition of form

2. Similar colour

3. Similar material

4. Metaphor

5. Style

6. Similar environment

Indexical sign references

1. The trace of a tool

2. A pointing form

3. Marks of use

4. Other kinds of traces

5. Light and sound signals

6. Sound of use and noise of a product

7. Smell of a product

8. Touch of the material

9. Graphic figures on the product form

Symbolic sign references

1. Graphic symbols

2. Symbolic colour

3. Symbolic forms

4. Symbolic positions and postures

5. Symbolic material

EXAMPLES OF PREVIOUS ANALYSES CONCERNING DESIGN PRODUCTS:

Barnes, W: Ein System elektromedizinischer Geräte. *form* 18, Zeitschrift für Gestaltung, Opladen, 1962, 40–45.

Bonsiepe, Gui: Analyse IBM 72 Selectric. *form* 17, Zeitschrift für Gestaltung, Opladen, 1962, 34–41.

Bonsiepe, Gui: Produktgrafik. *form* 28, Zeitschrift für Gestaltung, Opladen, 1964, 45–48.

Bonsiepe, Gui: Transport und Unterhaltung. Analyse Armaturentafeln in Automobilen. *form* 29, Zeitschrift für Gestaltung, Opladen, 1964, 38–45.

Bonsiepe, Gui: Ein Kühlschrank. *form* 30, Zeitschrift für Gestaltung, Opladen,1965, 24–29.

Bonsiepe, Gui: Analyse Taschenfeuerzeuge. *form* 33, Zeitschrift für Gestaltung, Opladen, 1966, 40–45.

Bonsiepe, Gui: Design-Analyse Messer, Gabel, Löffel. *form* 38, Zeitschrift für Gestaltung, Opladen 1967, 28–31.

Garnich, Rolf: Konstruktion Design Ästhetik. (Diss.) Selbstverlag, Stuttgart, 1968.

Klose, Odo und von Lieben, Hans: Drehwerkzeuge: Zehn Schraubendreher. *form* 40, Zeitschrift für Gestaltung, Opladen, 1967, 25–27.

Klose, Odo: 13 Montagesysteme. *form* 43, Zeitschrift für Gestaltung, Opladen, 1968, 19–25.

Klose, Odo: Auf der Suche nach der Form des Teeautomaten. *form* 113, Zeitschrift für Gestaltung, Seeheim, 1986, 44–45.

Klöcker, Ingo: Die Produkt-Form und menschliches Verhalten. Eine Untersuchung von psycho-physiologischen Ursachen und Wirkungen, Elementen und Kriterien der Gestaltung von Geräten, Maschinen, Anlagen und Fahrzeugen. (Diss.) Technische Universität Hannover, 1980.

Landry, Roch: Les rapports de l'homme aux objets: Etude d'un case choix des chaises droites. Université de Montréal, 1981.

Lindinger, Herbert: Analyse Nähmaschine. *form* 18, Zeitschrift für Gestaltung, Opladen, 1962, 32–42.

Rams, Dieter und Ullman, Roland: "Gute form ist nie vollendet". *form* 108/109, Zeitschrift für Gestaltung, Seeheim, 1984/85, 38–41.

Schricker, Erwin und Klose, Odo: Entwicklung eines Handstaubsaugers. *form* 18, Zeitschrift für Gestaltung, Opladen, 1962, 10–19.

Schürer, Arnold: Der Einfluss Produktbestimmender Faktoren auf die Gestaltung. (Diss. 1969) Selbstverlag, Bielefeld, 3. verbesserte Auflage, 1974.

Wolf, Brigitte: Design für den Alltag. (Diss.) Profil-Verlag, München, 1983.

A3

THE LIST OF STEAM IRONS IN A USER TEST AS PART OF CONSUMER RESEARCH (AALTO 1986), THE STEAM IRONS CHOSEN AS EXAMPLES FOR MY STUDY IN 1989, AND STEAM IRON MODELS ON THE MARKET IN HELSINKI IN 1994. TECHNICAL AND ERGONOMIC ASPECTS CONSIDERED AND MEASURED FOR THE SEMANTIC ANALYSIS (ALSO VIHMA 1990). PICTURES OF THE SAMPLE MATERIAL.

The list of the 12 steam irons chosen for my study on the left and the 4 comparable models analysed in the user test (Aalto 1986) on the right:

1.	AEG DB 402	AEG DB 403
2.	AEG DB 309	
3.	Braun PV 63	Braun PV 43
4.	Braun PV 64	comparable
5.	Moulinex 3600	
6.	Rowenta DA 21	Rowenta DA 21
7.	Rowenta DA 23	comparable
8.	Rowenta DA 32	comparable
9.	Rowenta DA 33	comparable
10.	Philips HD 1464	
11.	Philips HD 1462	
12.	Tefal Compact 15L	Tefal 10L

The steam iron models analysed in the user test (Aalto 1986), but not available on the market in 1988 anymore:

1.	AKA DE 203
2.	Hugin Variable
3.	Jura 360 (BC 2)
4.	Moulinex 773
5.	Nida FV 827
6.	Philips HD 1257
7.	Rowenta DA 49
8.	Siemens TB 76

New steam iron models by the same producers on the market in Helsinki in 1994:

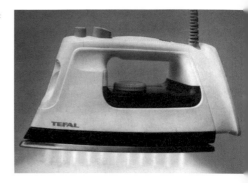

1. Braun Special PV 53
2. Braun ultra PV 73 S
3. Braun protector PV 74 S
4. Moulinex Chrono Jet B02
5. Moulinex Chrono Jet E07
6. Moulinex Chrono Jet SPC Vario Chrom Plus B82
7. Moulinex Ultimate 200/V56
8. Moulinex Ultimate 300/V58
9. Philips HD 1487 Comfort
10. Philips HD 1644 Comfort 460 'Aqua Cassette'
11. Rowenta DE-57 'Surfline'
12. Rowenta DE-211 'Clip-up'
13. Rowenta DE-223 'Clip-up'
14. Rowenta DE-11 'Trio'
15. Rowenta DE-19 'Trio'
16. Tefal Primo Supergliss Actif 20 (1418)
17. Tefal Ultragliss 20 (1600)

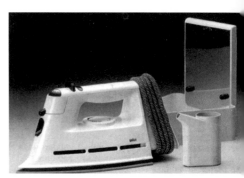

Technical and ergonomic data considered and measured for the semantic analysis of the sample material:

- size and form of the sole-plate
- materials of the sole-plate
- supply voltage W 1000–1100 (supply voltage of new models can be 1200-1300 W, and 1800 W in the case of the Moulinex Ultimate models)
- weight gr 1300–1400
- length mm 230–280
- width mm 117–125
- height mm 122–140
- water ml 200–250
- size of handle mm (length, width, height, measure round)

- indication of the amount of water in the tank
- location of thermostat
- location of push button for the water shower

- length and material of the cord

- manuals (content, form, languages, illustrations)

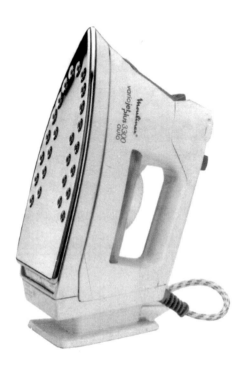

A4 TECHNICAL AND ERGONOMIC ASPECTS OF THE TUNTURI ECB PERFORMANCE ERGOMETER E 450 CYCLE (REGISTERED DESIGN) DESIGNED BY HEIKKI KIISKI, E&D DESIGN OY IN TURKU, FINLAND AND MADE BY TUNTURIPYÖRÄ OY, 1992–.

- length 96 cm
- width 62 cm
- height 111 cm
- weight 50 kg
- flywheel weight 19 kg

- silent, wear-free magnet brake
- LCD meter with simultaneous display of pulse, effort, time, energy consumption, distance, programmable pulse and effort limits, timer
- wide resistance adjustment range
  50 rpm/25-180 W
  100 rpm/55-410 W
- heavy flywheel for smooth pedalling
- comfortable seat height adjustment
- adjustable position of handlebars
- galvanized steel frame

The observations for the analysis of the E 450 were made at the Kuntorivakka training centre in September 1993. The cycle has been for sale in Helsinki during 1993–1995.

Examples of other models of exercise cycles during 1980-1995.

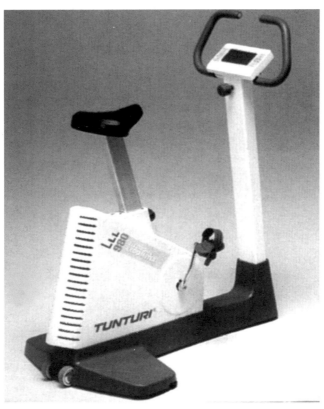

TECHNICAL AND ERGONOMIC ASPECTS OF THE M-89 KIOSK DESIGNED IN 1988 BY ARCHITECT JUHANI PALLASMAA AND DESIGNED FOR THE CITY OF HELSINKI ON COMMISSION OF THE HELSINKI TELEPHONE COMPANY.

- aluminium profile, glass (5 mm), wood, steel (basement of concrete)
- kiosk equipment: telephone, ceiling lamp (Philips FWN 12, softlight, 1x1W), door pump (Abloy 0024), wooden shelf on steel support, carpet (Norament 925 B), door handle (aluminium, 20 mm)

The following requirements should be considered in the design of the kiosk from the user's point of view:
- open form from underneath to help cleaning
- no screws in sight
- apparatus used by the telephone company must fit in (These three requirements were included in the commission.)
- protective against climatic conditions
- opening the door, the weight of the door (35 kg) and the form of the handle
- the floor surface
- the steps
- ventilation
- light
- acoustics
- a model according to wheel chair users' special measurements
- room for a handbag and the like

The kiosk was analysed outdoors in the centre of the city in September 1993.

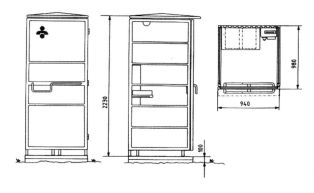

A6 TECHNICAL AND ERGONOMIC ASPECTS OF THE MET SKYMASTER HELMET MADE BY MET SRL, ITALY.

Skymaster has been IT-tested (International Testing) according to DIN 33954. The European standard (E DIN EN 1078) concerning bicycle helmets will be used in Finland from 1995.

- thermoplastic shell
- polystyrene inside
- adjustable chin strip
- sizes XS, S, M, L
- weight 250 gr
- colours: white, black, red and yellow; with two different decorations.

Other requirements from the user's point of view:
- measurement
- lock
- ventilation
- visibility in traffic
- cleaning

A white Skymaster helmet was bought and analysed at the premises of UIAH in September 1993.

Picture of other models of bicycle helmets on the market in Helsinki 1993-1995.

209